What is Military History?

What is
Military History?

Stephen Morillo
with Michael F. Pavkovic

polity

First published in 2006 by Polity Press

Reprinted in 2008, 2009

Polity Press
65 Bridge Street
Cambridge CB2 1UR, UK.

Polity Press
350 Main Street
Malden, MA 02148, USA

ISBN–10: 0–7456–3390–0
ISBN–13: 978–07456–3390–9
ISBN–10: 0–7456–3391–9 (pb)
ISBN–13: 978–07456–3391–6 (pb)

A catalogue record for this book is available from the British Library.

Typeset in 10.5 on 13 pt Sabon
by Carnegie Publishing Ltd, Lancaster
Printed and bound in the United States by Odyssey Press Inc.,
Gonic, New Hampshire

For further information on Polity, visit our website: www.politybooks.com

Contents

1

An Introduction to Military History

Military history is not the most respected branch of historical inquiry in academic circles. In part this is because of (and despite) its popularity with the general public and its importance in educating professional military personnel. The root of the disrespect, however, mostly lies in its subject: war. There exists deep suspicion that to write about war is somehow to approve of it, even to glorify it – a suspicion not unfounded in the history of the writing of military history. But to recognize the importance of a subject in the study of the past does not mean approving of it, as any historian of the Holocaust will attest. Military history today is practiced by as broad a range of historians, in their political, ideological, and methodological interests, as any other branch of history, and in both its topics and its methods lies (and should lie) solidly in the mainstream of historical study. This book is an introduction to this important field.

In most places, by the time writing was invented there were already kings and armies. It did not take long for kings to recognize the value of the new communication technology in publicizing and thus glorifying their exploits. Military victories proved especially useful for such publicity, as they demonstrated the ruler's capacity to protect his subjects, and to subject foreign populations with their riches to his rule (presumably to the benefit of the kingdom as a whole). Even more powerfully, the image of a war leader as presented in writing and pictures spoke directly of the very qualities most likely to enhance a ruler's reputation: strength, decisiveness, glory, even fearsomeness. A ruler with a good military publicist appeared favored by the gods.

Military history is therefore the oldest form of historical writing in many cultures. It has long since ceased to be the exclusive preserve of publicists for great leaders, although such types certainly still exist in abundance and the genre has produced some great literature, especially if one considers epics such as *The Iliad* as a form of military history. Indeed, it ceased to be the preserve of publicists in antiquity, when some of the finest minds in a number of classical civilizations turned to writing history, the history of wars in particular, partly in reaction to the tradition of heroic epics. Their more analytical approach to the study of history did not replace popular war tales, but coexisted with them. In both fictional and non-fictional forms, the appeal of writing about war remains. In many places today, military history continues to be one of the most popular sorts of history and of non-fiction generally. This popularity still extends beyond the written word, just as it did in the days of oral traditions of war tales such as *The Iliad:* the programming of The History Channel is dominated by military history.

Yet that very popularity means that there are many types of military history and a sometimes overwhelming volume of publications. The quality of this outpouring is inevitably uneven, and military history has not always enjoyed a high reputation in academic circles, for reasons we will explore further elsewhere in this book. The popularity of military history therefore complicates the problem of getting to know the field. Where does a beginning student of military history begin to understand this deep and complex tradition of historical writing? The intent of this book is to provide a beginners' road map: to introduce students to the history of military history, to its current forms, practitioners, audiences, and controversies, and to its key concepts and directions. In short, this book attempts to answer the question "What is Military History?"

We'll make an initial pass at this question from two angles. First, what is military history about? And second, who studies military history and why do they do so?

Military History: Definitions, Topics, Scope

We adopt a broad definition of military history. At the core of the field, of course, are histories of war – both particular wars and warfare (the conduct of military operations) more generally. But narratives of campaigns and battles, or even analyses of the patterns and principles of warfare illustrated by campaigns and battles, sometimes called the "art" or "science" of war, can be told in many ways. The historian can look at a war in terms of how it fits into the larger political aims of a country or leader, what strategies leaders adopted to fit their larger aims, how and how well those strategies were executed, or what the results of the war were – that is, histories of particular wars and warfare are part of the larger topic of histories of war in all its complex manifestations and effects. The focus at any of these levels might be on the decisions made by leaders, the institutions that put those decisions into operation, the experience of individuals far from the decision-making process but close to the action generated by the decisions, or the world of ideas, beliefs, and ideologies, including religious beliefs and practices, that shaped the plans, decisions, and actions of individuals and groups.

Nor do such varied approaches to the narration and analysis of warfare exhaust the possibilities of military history. Some armies never fight wars, but as institutions they are important (or simply interesting) despite (or even because of) the fact that they didn't fight. Military institutions, in other words, are as much the province of military history as are military actions. This is particularly true since institutional history subsumes the history of military organization, unit structures, and allocations of equipment. Likewise, the varying roles of soldiers and warriors in different societies and the social impact of warfare – whether directly through the interaction of combatants with non-combatants or indirectly through taxation, conscription, and other effects associated with the intrusion into societies of states and organized violence – have become central to much military history. The basic constraints placed on warfare and those who wage it by deep factors such as environment, climate, geography, and patterns of economic production as well as overall levels of economic productivity have also entered the mainstream of military history, especially in terms of histories of military technology. Technology, science, and the impact of war on individuals intersect in the history of military medicine. And the very popularity of war tales in many cultures indicates just one of the ways in which warfare, military institutions, and military values (including warrior codes of behavior) interact with the cultural values and constructs of different societies, bringing cultural analyses of war and warriors into the debate. Furthermore, both social structures and cultural constructs, including gender roles, affect the ways armies are raised, how they fight, and how they interact with society more broadly. In other words, the relationship between war and military institutions on one hand and society and culture on the other is reciprocal.

We therefore arrive at a broad definition of military history that encompasses not just the history of war and wars, but that includes any historical study in which military personnel of all sorts, warfare (the way in which conflicts are actually fought on land, at sea, and in the air), military institutions, and their various intersections with politics, economics, society, nature, and culture form the focus or topic of the work. One obvious implication of such a broad definition is that many works of military history could also be classified variously as political, economic, institutional, intellectual, social, or cultural history. Indeed the best history, military and otherwise, necessarily crosses many of these abstract academic boundaries in order to present as rich and rounded a view of the past as possible. In practice, military history has benefited from methodological advances and insights derived from other subfields of history, as well as from separate but related academic fields such as anthropology, sociology, and literary criticism.

Historiography is the study of the history of historical writing; one of its basic principles is that while histories can be divided by their central intellectual or topical approaches, the historical categories used are not clear and compartmentalized, but overlap across fuzzy boundaries. The categories themselves are invented – there is nothing "natural" or essential about them – and so over time their definitions and boundaries are frequently contested and adjusted.

One reason history gets divided up into subfields is for convenience of historiographical analysis. Historical writing really does fall into recognizable groupings, even if the groupings can be rearranged if viewed from a different angle, just as any set of historical data can be divided up depending on the interests of the particular historian. But another reason is that many of the practitioners of historical writing since the mid-nineteenth century have become increasingly professionalized in specific ways that contribute to specialization and subdivision. Historians working within academic institutions – colleges, universities, and research institutes – are especially prone to specify their areas of specialization for a variety of reasons that include the utility of such divisions for historical research in an age of ever-increasing information, but are also influenced by academic politics, the interests of sources for funding research, and the workings of academic job markets. The subfield of military history is further complicated by such dynamics because a significant amount of military history writing, because of its attraction to popular audiences, has always come from outside of academic institutions. This brings us to the question of military history's practitioners and audiences.

Who Studies Military History and Why?

The audiences for military history have changed over time, with significant implications for who has written military history and why. The audiences for military history in today's modern world generally fall into three major types. First is the popular audience, those readers in the general population who are interested in military history as recreational reading. This has long been and continues to be a large and therefore economically significant group – a mass market, at least potentially – whose attractions draw writers not just from among academics and professional military personnel but also from professional authors and popularizers who happen to choose military topics for their marketability.

Second is the academic audience. We include in this category both professional academics whose specialty is military history and who read to keep up with developments in the field and in support of their own research and writing, and students at both the undergraduate and graduate level whose reading of military history is (presumably) more focused and guided than that of the popular audience and is directly related to advancement in their academic careers. In this category, the audience and the practitioners, that is those who write military history, are often the same people, though the most influential military history writing usually appeals to both a scholarly or academic audience and to a popular audience. Success in "crossing over" from a purely academic audience to a mass popular audience can influence the academic careers of authors: John Keegan, one of the most successful academic historians to reach the mass market, eventually gave up his teaching post at Sandhurst Military Academy to write full time. Moreover, the "mass market" appeal of military history, even in the academic world, can be seen in the robust enrollments often seen in courses that deal with the study of war and the military.

Keegan's academic position illustrates the overlap of the academic world with the third audience for military history: professional military personnel for whom knowledge of military history is not simply an academic specialty of choice but, at least theoretically, a qualification for the demands of their job. In addition to academics, military specialists and authors from the ranks of government and in quasi-academic institutions ("Think Tanks" and the like) write for this audience. As a result, some of this literature is more technical and practice-oriented (though not necessarily less theoretically informed) than purely academic military history tends to be, as it is likely to have the most direct impact on the making of military policy and the implementation of military action by states and their armies. On the other hand, to bring this introductory discussion of practitioners and audiences full circle, a traditional sort of military history author has been the retired military officer who uses the credibility of both his military experience and his advertisable rank as entryways to the mass popular market. Though less common now than it was 50 years ago, the image of the "retired general" as author continues to inform the popular image of military history among both mass and academic audiences, with varying effects. Keegan, for example, felt it necessary to explain, in his Introduction to *The Face of Battle*, what he could bring to military history despite his lack of direct military experience.

The practical uses of military history for professional military personnel and the civilian governments that direct military activity today provide the clearest and most direct illustration of an important and general historiographical principle: that the questions historians ask about the past, in this case about past military actions, institutions, and so forth, are crucially shaped by their present concerns and perspectives. In other words, military history, like all history, is a dialogue between past and present. Because the present is constantly changing, views of the past change constantly as well. In the mid-1980s through the beginning of the twenty-first century, professional military history in the United States, those discussions among and aimed at military practitioners and policy makers, was dominated by the notion of a Revolution in Military Affairs (which we will discuss at more length in chapter 4 below) that focused on high technology and its effect on the "battlefield of the future," that evanescent place that changes in harness with the ever-changing present. The combined effects, however, of the September 11, 2001, terrorist attack on the World Trade Center and the problematic nature of the US occupation of Iraq in the wake of rapid battlefield "victory" have increasingly shifted attention to the problems associated with irregular warfare against unconventional, non- or quasi-military enemies, problems not obviously liable to high-tech solutions but intimately related to complex questions of ideology, civil society and its relation to military manpower, and the role of the military, while a renewed threat (and reality) of nuclear proliferation in Iran, North Korea, and possibly elsewhere has raised the profile of issues including diplomacy and force and strategic deployment of limited military resources. In short, the impact of Gulf War I on American military thought, with its emphasis on high technology and tactics, has been overshadowed by the more recent impact of 9/11 and the Iraq War in which high-tech and conventional tactics seem much less relevant, and the emphasis of professional military history has shifted in response.

This shift has obvious implications for the sorts of historical evidence historians engaged in these debates will bring to bear on their arguments. The relevant historical parallels and examples in the debate over the Revolution in Military Affairs involved other supposed cases of rapid technological and tactical change, especially the spread of gunpowder weaponry in sixteenth-century Europe (again, this is discussed at more length in chapter 4). But the current debate looks much more to colonial wars in the nineteenth century, guerilla wars of the mid-twentieth century, and even classical examples of imperial powers such as Rome dealing with "barbarian" neighbors and rebellious provincials. Such cases are chosen to gain insight into a contemporary situation in which disparities of technology and force do not have the same impact that they have had on the conventional battlefields of the past, including those cases highlighted by the earlier debate, and in which social and cultural factors seemingly outweigh traditional political relationships between states.

In both debates, however, the historical cases chosen as evidence for one argument or another are subject to rejection, reinterpretation, or revision by other historians who either see the problems of the present differently or see the crucial characteristics of the past differently, or both. Both debates, for instance, are much more central to military history published in the United States than elsewhere, since the concerns of other states that are neither the undisputed leaders in military technology nor likely to be seen as a new global Roman Empire are different from those of the US, which fits both criteria. Historians who do not share those concerns will bring a different perspective to both debates or will engage in other debates entirely.

Presented with this sort of endlessly qualified and complicated academic arguing, with its multiple interpretations, ways of looking at evidence, methodologies, and perspectives, some students are apt to throw up their hand and conclude that "it's all just opinion" and give up on history as being able to teach any lessons. But it isn't just "all opinion." There are, for starters, better and worse uses and abuses of evidence, and all branches of historical inquiry remain empirically grounded in evidence. But more importantly, even if historical data prove incapable of decisively answering a current question (history never, after all, exactly repeats itself, though, as Mark Twain once said, it does rhyme), the fact that historians have, as a result of current concerns, asked new questions about the past leads to new understandings of the past. This is in part because not all interpretations of the past are mutually exclusive: most, in fact, are complementary, and the more of them we have, the more nuanced is our understanding of the past. This is a nice result even if it makes drawing lessons from such complex understandings even harder (since lessons often need to be simple to be applicable).

In short, history, including military history, can be used to entertain; it can contribute to and advance academic careers, it can even perhaps teach lessons. But above all, given the prevalence of military activity in the past actions of humanity, it can help us understand the past and how we got to where we are today, even if the implications of that route for the future remain necessarily contentious.

Overview of this Book

We may summarize the previous two sections of this introduction by way of a photographic metaphor. If the past (in this case the part of the past connected to military activity) is the *subject of the picture* an historian creates, different approaches to the *methodology* of military history can be likened to the different *lenses* a photographer might use. An army looks different through an economic or social lens from the way it appears through a cultural or institutional lens. But the choice of a particular topic or approach depends on the interests of the historian and the interests of the intended audience for the history. A history written by and for professional staff officers will differ from one written for popular or academic readers. This can be thought of as the *perspective* of the photographer, the angle or location from which the picture is taken. (As this metaphor tries to make clear, every historian necessarily has a perspective: just as a photographer has to be *somewhere* to take a picture, an historian has to be *somewhere*, metaphorically, to write history. There is no such thing as omnisciently objective history. But perspective is *not* the same as *bias*. Bias results when an historian uses a particular perspective purposely to distort or exclude from view aspects of the subject necessary for understanding it. Different perspectives can be mutually complementary, building a better overall understanding of the subject. Different biases conflict unproductively, reducing understanding.)

The changing combinations of lenses and perspective that historians have brought to bear on the military past have produced the characteristics of military history that the rest of this book will explore in more detail. Chapter 2 traces the history of the writing of military history. How did military history come to be the field that it is today? Where did it start, and how has it evolved and changed over time? Chapter 3 explores the key concepts and theories that shape the study of military history currently. Chapter 4 extends this examination to some important or representative controversies in the field, showing what military historians are arguing about and why they do so. Chapter 5 discusses how military history is done, ranging from the sources military historians use and the forms in which it is presented to the places where it is taught and the key outlets for academic military history. Finally, chapter 6 looks at the future of military history. Where is it going? What is its relevance in the wider world of the twenty-first century?

A book this brief cannot possibly answer the question "What is Military History?" exhaustively. Inevitably, we'll miss some things and cover others too lightly. But we hope to provide newcomers to the field with a reliable roadmap that will make further explorations more comprehensible and thus more enjoyable.

2
Military Historiography

As we noted in chapter 1, military history is one of the oldest fields of historical writing. In this chapter, we will trace the history of military history – the historiography of the field – from its origins down to the present. This chapter therefore answers several important questions about military history: Where did it start? How has it evolved and changed over time? What influenced and shaped those changes? In short, how did military history come to be the field that it is today?

The same questions of audience and purpose that we began to explore in chapter 1, set in changing contexts of warfare, have shaped the writing of military history in all eras and places. Early military literature tended to lie somewhere on a continuum defined by two different sorts of audiences and purposes. At one pole of this continuum we find heroic war tales, often originally oral in form, told for the entertainment of warriors themselves. This sort of military literature was especially prevalent in societies with weak or divided states dominated by warrior elites. At the other pole we find formal analyses of warfare written for the didactic or propagandistic benefit of the rulers either of strong states or of those wishing to become so. This form was less common than war tales, as strong states were not so common in the ancient world, but retains more influence in modern writing of military history. This accounts for the geographical focus of this survey, for two major analytic traditions with lasting influence emerged, one in the Greco-Roman world and one in the Chinese world. Ultimately, the academic intellectual tradition of Western Europe that descended from elements of the Greco-Roman tradition and flourished in the emerging nation-states of nineteenth-century Europe has come to dominate military history today. What thus might appear to be a Euro-centric bias is simply a reflection (though not necessarily an unproblematic one) of the historiographic record.

Classical Roots:
Military History in Ancient Times

Militarily oriented "deeds of kings" have arisen in almost every complex society with a written language, from ancient Sumer and Egypt to Mayan Mesoamerica and ancient China. Aimed at polishing the reputation of rulers and, perhaps, providing instruction to their successors, they inform modern military history only as sources, not as models of historiography. And orally transmitted war tales undoubtedly existed even before kings and states, though we only know of those that entered a written tradition. Homer's *Iliad* is, in the western tradition, the foundational example of this type. These, too, are useful today mainly as sources, but are perhaps even more difficult as sources than are royal propaganda. For royal propaganda, though it often distorted the events it recounted, did so in fairly predictable ways and related recent events, whereas oral traditions can preserve elements of distant events and systems, but in distorted and miscontextualized ways that can be very hard to untangle. Military history that informs modern writing as more than source material therefore begins, in the West, with the Greeks of the fifth century BCE.

The Greeks

History emerged in Greece as one form of rational inquiry about the world, and was thus part of the general intellectual flowering that is associated particularly with fifth-century

Athens. The Greeks saw history as, like medicine, a search for causes of current events (though as in medicine and other areas of Greek life, rationality coexisted with "irrational" and religious traditions that have often been underemphasized), and also as a rhetorical art for conveying its findings comparable to drama, philosophy, and poetry. And like much of the political and intellectual flowering of this time, history reflected the division of Greece into many small city-states that were endemically at war with each other and took as its initial inspiration a military event: the defeat of the Persian invasions of 490 and 481 by a rare coalition of those city-states.

As a result, in terms of purpose and audience the writing of history was closely bound up, especially in Athens, with the politics of Athenian democracy and the naval empire Athens built in the second half of the fifth century. Politics (which externally almost always meant war or coercion) was a matter of public debate and decision-making; political participation was closely linked with service in the hoplite phalanx (for better-off, landowning citizens) and in the trireme navy (for poorer, landless citizens). Historians' accounts of past wars in the case of Herodotus, and in the case of Thucydides current ones, as well as the actual experience of battle for most citizens in a *polis*, would have formed part of the stock of knowledge available to voters and debaters in the public assembly about military tactics, strategy, diplomacy, the ethics of warfare, and indeed of the process of running a war democratically. Athenian defeat in the Peloponnesian War at the end of the fifth century altered this political context somewhat, but it survived for some of the fourth century, while militarily an increase in mercenary service among Greeks during and after the Peloponnesian War provides the background for the military memoirs and analysis of Xenophon, among others.

Two major figures dominate Greek historiography in this period: the aforementioned Herodotus and Thucydides. Each established approaches to writing history that have influences and analogues down to the present. And for each, war was *the* great subject of history: Herodotus wrote his history of the Persian Wars "to show how [the Greeks and Persians] came into conflict";[1] Thucydides wrote about the Peloponnesian War "in the belief that it was going to be a great war and more worth writing about than any of those which had taken place" in past ages that were "not great periods in warfare or in anything else."[2] But in their method and framework of analysis they differed significantly.

Herodotus constructs a drama whose main characters are entire peoples: the Persians, the Greeks ("our people"), and others including Egyptians and Scythians who were subject to or fought against the Persians. He portrays these characters ethnographically and anthropologically, analyzing the effect of their geographical setting and climate, mining a range of oral and written sources including drama and poetry that offer insights into what the essential traits and motives of a people were. Heroic deeds by individuals are there, but in a context that gives them meaning. Long out of modern favor for not being "scientific" and critical about his sources (and suffering by comparison with Thucydides from his non-soldier's credulity about battle details), Herodotus and his cultural take on warfare more recently look conceptually chic in light of the recent rise of cultural history and interdisciplinary studies (discussed further in chapter 3).

Thucydides, by contrast, places warfare more narrowly in a political framework of analysis, and explicitly rejects Herodotus' (and others') reliance on the evidence of "poets" and "mythology,"[3] writing instead from "the plainest evidence" – his own or others' eyewitness reports, preferably – cross-checked whenever possible. (On the other hand, Herodotus identifies his sources, whereas Thucydides does not, specifically.) He probably looks more modern and scientific than he really was methodologically, but at least established an ideal. In terms of the content of military history, he set high standards for the analysis of how strategy must fit political goals and available resources, of the difficult moral choices that face individuals and states in wartime, and of the interaction of individual psychology and the dynamics of battle. His description of how phalanxes tend to drift rightwards as "fear makes every man want to do his best to find protection for his unarmed side in the shield of the man next to him" in the advance is justly famous.[4] Moreover, his net assessment of the length of the war and what was needed to win were outstanding examples of the Clausewitzian relationship between political objective and military strategy.

Xenophon, an Athenian born at the beginning of the Peloponnesian War and an admirer of Socrates, contributed to a version of the Thucydidean line of military history. A country gentleman who joined a band of 10,000 Greek mercenaries fighting for a pretender to the Persian throne in 401, he became a military leader during the expedition and went on to a career as a commander and writer. The *Anabasis*, his account of the 401–399 campaign, has something of the character of a veteran soldier's memoirs and lacks Thucydides' keen political insights, but contains detailed tactical analysis and descriptions as well as perceptive commentary on leadership. He went on to write much philosophy and history, including the *Hipparchicus* on cavalry command (both his sons became cavalry commanders), much of which has a strongly moral and religious theme.[5]

Xenophon's career as a mercenary points to the political changes that affected the Greek world after the Peloponnesian War. Citizen armies declined in importance, and by the 330s Greece fell under the hegemonic rule of Philip of Macedon and his son Alexander. Alexander's conquests inspired kings and generals for generations to come, but also cemented the political transformation of what now became the Hellenistic world – a world of Greek culture spread widely over a vast Empire that after Alexander's death broke into numerous competing kingdoms. The local politics of individual Greek city-states were definitively eclipsed by sumptuous royal courts attended by an educated elite drawn from all over the Hellenistic world. Alexander's example and the need on the part of his successors' dynasties for ideological support led to the development of cults of royal personality as well as conspicuous display in the deployment of military force – elephants and huge, unwieldy warships both feature prominently in Hellenistic warfare. The growing professionalism of Hellenistic armies also led to the development of treatise-based military literature. Much of this literature focused on the technical elements of military organization, tactics, and drill, but it also analyzed strategy and tactics by drawing on examples from earlier times.

The culmination of the Greek tradition of military history was embodied in the history of Rome's rise at the expense of the Hellenistic world as related by Polybius. Although he came to Rome as a hostage, Polybius eventually came under the protection and patronage of some of Rome's leading families, notably the Scipios. He was thus able to write a history of Roman expansion, including discussions of the Roman political and military systems, that is a model, at least in the ancient world, of objectivity and detailed and reliable research.

In this atmosphere, the analytic traditions of Thucydides and Herodotus receded in favor of praise of rulers' glorious deeds. Alexander's many biographers, including his generals and successors such as Ptolemy I of Egypt, set the tone for this style of writing, and biographies of commanders became a favorite mode of military historical writing. Accounts followed actual warfare in settling into formulaic patterns of narrative and action. Battle descriptions remained detailed, but the detail tended not to vary significantly. And analysis of warfare receded somewhat in historical writing in favor of "insider" accounts of court politics and intrigue. The audience seems to have been limited to elites, and very few Hellenistic histories survive in original form: we know about them mostly from summaries or excerpts in Roman historical writing. For both politically and historiographically the Romans were the heirs of the Hellenistic world.

The Romans

Roman historical experience began on a Greek model of a small city-state fielding citizen armies against its neighbors. This context gave birth to an interlocked set of values that would have resonance in Roman historical writing long after they ceased to apply in practical terms to much of the Roman population, since the growing Roman state eventually made a transition from a Republic to an Empire that owed much to Hellenistic styles of rulership. Even under the Empire, however, Romans saw virtue as intimately tied to military participation, which in turn was very closely tied to citizenship. Military values and a warrior ethos thus pervaded Roman culture and politics. But beyond this, Republican Rome was not especially an engine of cultural innovation. Historical writing mostly came late to Rome via Greek models, after Rome's conquest of Greece and Macedon in the second century BCE. It thus matured by the late Republic, in a context characterized by the transition from citizen militia armies to long-service professionals, by increasing levels of civil war, and ultimately by the transition to Empire under Augustus. Thenceforth, the context for military historical writing in Rome was a system in which the army dominated, military virtues were enshrined in a vast organization that encouraged a kind of Professional Military Education, and unstable dynastic politics encouraged emphasis on heroic military leadership at the top of the system. The audience for military history in Rome thus consisted, for most of its history, of an educated elite with both military and civic duties, and increasingly later a group of professional military men with command responsibilities (and often political ambitions).

Undoubtedly the most influential writer of Roman military history was himself a major participant: Julius Caesar. His detailed accounts of his campaigns in and conquest of Gaul[6] and then his victory in civil war[7] formed part of his own self-promotion in the context of competition for leadership of the Roman state. But he was as skillful a writer as he was a general, and so the style of analysis he used to describe his campaigns and battles has had a tremendous impact on military history writing in the western tradition ever since. He certainly glorifies himself and his role in the wars he conducted. But he embedded his claim to greatness in apparently dispassionate analysis of what actually happened – it just turned out that what actually happened shows Caesar to be a genius! He accomplished this trick by adapting the Greek tradition of detailed campaign and battle narratives to his purposes. He tells about the course of battles (and sieges) in detail. But unlike Thucydides and Xenophon, for whom the dynamics of battle were windows onto individual and mass psychology, warfare for Caesar was an intellectual art dominated by the mind of the general (himself). Caesar in effect made himself (and his opposing commander) the only active agent in a battle; his soldiers are reduced to automata (though often individually heroic ones in performing their duties) who carry out their leader's clever plans. It is largely from Caesar, in other words, that the main contours of the long western historiographical emphasis on the Art of Generalship (or the history of Great Captains) derive.

Among other Roman historians, Plutarch (actually a Greek moralizer who wrote about famous Greeks and Romans) and Suetonius follow Caesar's biographical lead, writing lives of great men who influenced Greek and Roman history, though Plutarch presents both positive and negative examples of leadership.[8] Sallust, a friend of Caesar's, traced the decline of Republican institutions, including a fine analysis of the generalship of Gaius Marius, whose reforms of the army made it a professional force. The two best-known historians, Livy and Tacitus, wrote general histories of Rome that might well be characterized as distant precursors to the nationalist histories of the nineteenth century (see below), as they construct a Roman history around the virtues of the Roman people with a significant dose of chauvinism about the peoples Rome fought and conquered. Neither was a soldier, but both were involved in politics; their military accounts are therefore often conventional, though Tacitus is particularly good at analyzing the strategic challenges faced by the early Empire and assessing how various rulers responded to them. Josephus, on the other hand, was a Jew who reluctantly joined the Jewish revolt of 70 CE, was captured and became a Roman advisor, and wrote an excellent history of the revolt that contrasts Roman and Jewish motivations very nicely and pays close attention to the human costs of war. Also a soldier was the later Roman historian Ammianus Marcellinus, who offers a wealth of reliable military detail and a more even-handed approach to non-Roman peoples than his predecessors, perhaps reflecting both his Greek origins and the more multi-ethnic composition of the later Empire. All the Roman historians write with clear political agendas. This conception of history as rhetorical argument combined with the Caesarian concept of generalship to produce a common trope of Roman battle writing, the pre-battle oration by the commander. Thucydides' focus on the connection of war and politics continued in Roman historiography, and Herodotus' ethnographic approach has echoes in both Tacitus and Ammianus.[9]

A final sort of Roman military writing was the military manual, or guidebook to being a successful general. Interestingly, the most famous example is the *Epitoma rei militaris* of Vegetius,[10] which dates to the late fourth century when the

Roman army was in a state of decline (or at least transformation). Vegetius explains principles of strategy, which are largely logistically based, tactical tricks, and above all stresses the need for and methods of recruiting soldiers and training them in close order drill. This sort of military writing, the Roman version of Professional Military Education, would have a long history in Byzantium and close analogues in China, as we shall see.

China

Historical and military writing of an analytic sort comparable to the best produced by Greeks and Romans emerged in China during the Warring States period (474–221 BCE). As in Greece, this was a time both of intense warfare and of political competition between multiple states (though Chinese states were always larger than Greek city-states) and intellectual ferment – the age of Confucius and many rival schools of philosophy – that focused on a search for order in the cosmos and in human affairs. Political order for many thinkers meant an end to intra-Chinese warfare and a return to the unity of an earlier age. In the course of the Warring States period, the number of states began to decrease steadily as bigger and better-organized states swallowed smaller and less efficient ones. This territorial consolidation was accompanied by significant changes in the internal political structure of the successful states. Previously dominated by a violent warrior aristocracy whose values find many echoes in the military virtues of Greece and Rome, Chinese civilization now saw the rise of a bureaucratic autocracy that increasingly monopolized the legitimate use of violence, focusing it in state-supplied mass conscript infantry armies at the expense of the old chariot- and horse-riding aristocrats. A class of bureaucrats dependent on state positions gradually came to be the most important social class, while rulers positioned themselves ideologically as the exclusive focal point for maintaining cosmic harmony and political order. Eventually the state of Qin unified all of China; the Han dynasty that followed after two Qin rulers formalized the imperial system.

On the way to unification, a number of analysts wrote

guides to the effective use of military force aimed at the rulers and their generals who were fighting the wars of the Warring States period. After unification, a separate tradition of historical writing emerged, the official dynastic history. The role of military history in both sorts of writing presents interesting contrasts and parallels with the Greek and Roman traditions.

Sunzi's *Art of War*[11] is the best known (and most completely preserved) of a number of similar military manuals that parallel the military manuals from the Hellenestic period and Vegetius and his ilk in the Greco-Roman world. They lay out very similar strategic principles (the similarity resulting from the same logistical constraints), advise on tactics, and recommend training methods. But there are differences. Sunzi draws explicitly on many more historical examples from Chinese history to illustrate his principles. More importantly, the emphasis throughout the manuals is on the crucial and central role of an intelligent general to military success. This has echoes of Caesar, but intelligence for Sunzi meant familiarity with the written principles he lays out, not the sort of intuitive genius Caesar attributes to himself. And if Caesar's soldiers appear as automata, they were at least ones accorded heroism and allowed, especially at the unit commander level, a significant measure of initiative. Sunzi's soldiers were supposed to be automata, period. Heroism was actively discouraged, and initiative was constructed as subversive of the general's control of the army. The ideological connection of this emphasis to the growth of political autocracy in Chinese states shows how military writing responded to and in turn shaped the political culture of societies. Unlike in Rome, where a warrior ethos pervaded a large, professionalized, and bureaucratically backed army, in China that same ethos was systematically ground out of existence along with the warrior aristocracy that had created it, in order to eliminate the aristocracy's threat to the ruling dynasty. Military action as a thing glorious in itself ceased to exist in Chinese ideology: it was reduced simply to a tool of state.

This writing of anti-military values continued in the historical tradition founded by the great Han dynasty historian Sima Qian.[12] He was a government historian with a place at court and access to all official government archives, and was a match for Thucydides at rational analysis and cross-checking of sources. And like the Greeks and Romans, he wrote history as morality and rhetoric: he wrote the history of the preceding (Qin) dynasty to legitimize the dynastic change to the Han. And to the ideological inclination of the military manuals against heroism he added a Confucian concern for humanity, good government, and maintenance of peace. His history of military affairs, which set a consistent pattern for Chinese historians thereafter, stressed strategic options to conflict and the political and moral lessons of wars, but paid little attention to the details of campaigns and almost none to the tactical course of battles, as the glory that such details might reflect was somewhere between irrelevant and dangerous. Results were all that mattered, and the key moral was that one might win an empire from horseback, but one could not rule from the saddle. The result is a tradition that to the military historian used to Greco-Roman style is frustratingly short of detail, though often just as good or better on institutional arrangements and the values underlying military action.

Military History in the Traditional World: Histories, Manuals, and War Tales

The break-up of Han China in 220 and the western half of the Roman Empire in the later fifth century, as well as the rise of Islam from 630, introduced significant changes to the context for military writing. The three main types established in the classical traditions – histories, manuals, and war tales – shared the stage in different ways in the various civilizations of the period *c*.400–1500.

Medieval Europe

The division of the western Roman Empire into barbarian kingdoms that had neither the economic nor the administrative strength of Rome accompanied the rise of Christianity and a social shift toward a more powerful independent military aristocracy as the major changes in the context for military writing in Europe between 400 and 1000. The sources reflect these changes, especially the dominance of the warrior elite and the concentration of learning in the Church.

History writing was poor by Roman standards. Intelligent analysis was rare, and many histories were little more than monastic chronicles or annals: basically lists of periodic (yearly) entries noting major events with little description. Even more narrative sources give little detail, especially military details about battles, as the concentration of history writing among monks meant that universal and ecclesiastical history predominated. The details that do come to us about battles are often lifted word-for-word and in whole paragraphs from classical Roman sources (knowledge of Greek was rare among writers during this period), meaning the details they do give are unreliable in describing the events they purport to cover, demonstrating the author's erudition in preference to his accuracy. Notions of causation also tend to reduce to "God's will": leadership in battle ceases to be a matter of brilliant generalship and instead becomes a test of piety.[13]

Similarly, no new military manuals were created. Copies of Vegetius survive in fair numbers, but the actual use of his work by practicing commanders is open to question. What thrived was an oral tradition of epic poetic war tales, some of which – notably the Song of Roland[14] – began to be written down as the period drew to a close. These poems reflect a world dominated by warrior elites and their heroic values, and find numerous parallels in other parts of the traditional world, from the *Sundiata* of West Africa to the war tales of Kamakura Japan.[15] They tend to tell tales of bravery, loyalty, and martial skill in colorful detail which, like the much earlier *Iliad*, reflects reality in complex and often misleading ways.

With the turn of the millennium, Western Europe's economy revived, royal power recovered, and warrior aristocratic culture was consolidated into the form of chivalry. Literacy and learning also revived, based on wider knowledge of a broader range of classical authors. Churchmen continued to predominate among history writers, but monks now shared the stage with clerics employed at royal courts, and both were increasingly joined by lay writers with different outlooks and experience.

The number of interesting histories therefore increased. A notable early group of historians were associated with the

Anglo-Norman realm created by William the Conqueror's conquest of England in 1066. William's own biographer William of Poitiers used Caesar's language to compare William favorably to the great Roman. Over the next 60 years historians, including Orderic Vitalis and William of Malmesbury, wrote lengthy and discerning histories of the period with a focus on England and Normandy and, in Orderic's case, the Crusades, which spawned their own set of historians.[16] Classicizing language remained common (Orderic described Turks using terms for Roman military units and formations, for example), but greater originality emerged. Local chronicles remained common and grew more detailed. By the fourteenth century the Hundred Years War saw the emergence of herald-historians such as Jean Froissart, who held quasi-official positions as the publicists of aristocratic deeds of chivalry, their roles recognized by both sides of many conflicts.[17] The product of a transregional aristocratic culture, their accounts are long on heroism and often short on the nuts and bolts of everyday military organization and the experience of despised common soldiers. Among all authors, notions of God's will as the ultimate cause of events remained, but writers explored proximate causes in human actions much more. The dominance of aristocratic values and outlooks also militated against professional manuals: Vegetius remained popular to copy but little used in practice and was not imitated. War tales moved from the epic style toward romance, as in the many versions of the Arthur story, and so drifted away from the historical tradition.

Byzantium

Roman traditions of statecraft and warfare survived alongside Greek culture more continuously in the eastern Empire, transformed by external threat and Islamic conquests into what historians call the Byzantine Empire. The imperial court at Constantinople dominated the intellectual life of the Empire, an aspect of the division between capital and provinces that shaped much Byzantine historical development. The educated civil aristocrats who served the imperial bureaucracy formed both the producers and the audience for historical literature, with churchmen playing a far less significant role than in Western Europe. And armed force remained more an institution of the state than the expression of aristocratic dominance that it was in the West.

The effect of this context on history writing was mixed. The civil orientation of the aristocracy in Constantinople meant that histories tended to focus on palace politics and the personalities of rulers. They are typified at either end of high Byzantine history by Procopius' portraits of the world of Justinian in the later sixth century and the royal biographies of Michael Psellos in the mid-eleventh and the learned and insightful history written by Anna Komnena, daughter of Emperor Alexios I, in the early twelfth.[18] Military events, the domain of provincial affairs and families, often received short shrift, and the writing of histories in general became somewhat sporadic, eclipsed by literary genres with more prestige such as philosophy. All Byzantine literature, including history, was produced in imitation of the language and style of classical Athenian models. On the other hand, the continued existence of a professional army encouraged the production of military manuals. They tended to be of good quality and to adapt to changing times, though the correspondence between written theory and actual practice is unclear in all cases. Emperors themselves wrote such guidebooks for their successors. They included both strategic and ethnographic information about the various states and peoples who bordered the Empire and how to deal with them diplomatically, advice on how to conduct campaigns against invading foreign armies superior in numbers to Byzantine defenders, and detailed tactical advice about the conduct of battles.[19] Finally, the cultural divide between capital and provinces resulted in the emergence of at least a few epic poetic war tales among the military families of the frontiers.[20] The disruption and decline of the Byzantine state after 1204 gradually brought an end to Byzantine historical writing and, in 1453, Byzantine history.

Islam

The fairly sudden appearance of an Arab empire in the form of the Islamic caliphate is remarkably poorly documented.

Outsiders didn't write much about it, and Arab literary traditions, mostly poetic before the conquests and then focused on the development of Islam itself afterwards, included few precedents for history writing. A Muslim-Arabic tradition of historical writing therefore took almost a century to emerge, and matured in contentious conditions. Scholars and caliphs struggled for ideological control of Islam, and Muslim military systems developed along a path of increasing separation from society.

Arab history writing therefore concentrated first on constructing an acceptable history of early Islam, and, like Western European and Byzantine history in this period, often paid scant attention to the details of military action. Also as in Europe, the will of Allah overshadowed human agency in causal explanations. But military manuals were produced regularly, and when the historical tradition matured in the age of the Crusades and then the Mongol invasions, the Muslim world produced some excellent historians, including Ibn al-Athir,[21] whose universal history contains notable accounts of the Third Crusade in 1189 and the Mongol invasions of the mid-thirteenth century. And then there is Ibn Khaldun, who lived in Spain and North Africa in the fourteenth century. His *Muqaddima*,[22] the historiographical and theoretical introduction to a planned world history, is perhaps the most sophisticated piece of historical writing between Thucydides and Edward Gibbon. His analysis of the dynamic between settled and nomadic peoples, though it clearly reflects the peculiar relationship between the two that had developed in the Islamic world in which nomads were the consistent source of political rejuvenation and legitimacy, is both psychologically perceptive and grounded in analysis of the impact of geography and social structure. For whatever reason, however, he had few followers in his or any other tradition.

China

The impact of the Han Empire's break-up after 220 was less transformative for the context of historical writing than the fall of the western Roman Empire had been. Though the state was divided, Chinese civilization had greater underlying continuity in its social and cultural structures, and by 589 the Empire had been reunited under the Sui and then Tang dynasties. The Tang was more militaristic in outlook and its aristocracy had many ties to steppe nomad horse-warriors, but neither Confucian values nor newly popular Buddhism provided frameworks for turning this militarism into an historiographical transformation. Even military rulers such as the first Tang emperor presented themselves in official depictions, both historical and pictorial, as Confucian scholars. Chinese traditions of historical writing established by Sima Qian therefore continued and developed along established lines. The period did see the emergence, however, of fictional romances with significant historical content – China's version of war tales, though significantly this was always a written tradition and its heroes were not warrior aristocrats but hero-commoners and even barbarians. Subsequent dynastic changes and even Mongol conquest did little to affect the Chinese historiographical tradition.

Europe from Renaissance to Enlightenment

A major set of disruptions in the fourteenth and fifteenth centuries did, on the other hand, bring change to the European historiographical tradition. These included the Black Death of 1348 (which had also struck China in the 1330s and killed Ibn Khaldun's father in the 1340s), the destruction attendant on the spreading Hundred Years War, religious instability and schism, and various economic and political crises. The cultural result of this century-long period of disruption was, generally speaking, to cause increased questioning of established traditions and the creation of new forms of expression. This tendency was reinforced by the influx into Italy of Greek scholars fleeing the collapsing Byzantine Empire in the early 1400s, where their trove of classical Greek texts contributed to the emphasis of the Renaissance on the study of classical literature including histories. The printing press allowed an explosion after 1453 of printed material. At the same time, the spread of gunpowder technology and the reorganization of the social and economic underpinnings of war-making produced a long period of experimentation and flux in military practice, while from about 1500 royal power recovered from the crisis to reach new heights of ambition and conflict militarily.

Military writing benefited. Machiavelli is a key figure. His works, which cross the boundaries of history and political science, include *The Prince*, *The Art of War*, and the *Discourses on Livy*.[23] They show the influence of classical works on the connection between politics and military affairs in their realistic analysis of how things are rather than how they ought to be. By the sixteenth and early seventeenth centuries, the continuity of some states combined with political disputes connected to the Wars of Religion, or in England the tension between Parliament and kings, to send historians to government archives searching for documents to provide precedents for their positions. But the real explosion in military writing, related in part to the emergence of standing army units in some states, came in the form of new military manuals. These were largely technical works: manuals, based on classical models, detailing drill with handguns, copiously illustrated; mathematically based treatises on the new geometric style of fortification designed to resist cannonade; recipes for gunpowder; and ballistics tables for gunners. But they also included a growing set of soldiers' memoirs and popular historical writing. Military history, like military manpower, weaponry, and logistics in Europe during this period, moved toward a more market-oriented merchant capitalist model.

From about 1660 a new set of transformations provided further impetus to change. The scientific revolution of the mid-seventeenth century promised further advances in military technology and began to demonstrate the possibilities of the mathematical-experimental method. The end of the Wars of Religion both eased religious tension, shifting cultural attention to the new science, and assisted in a new phase of the expansion of state power under both absolutist regimes as in the France of Louis XIV and constitutional polities such as England and the Netherlands. Greater state power was reflected in larger, more centrally controlled armies organized into permanent regiments that began to develop their own traditions, as well as in standing navies that extended the effective military reach of European military power to coasts around the world. Navies operated in tandem with merchant marines that bound emerging colonial empires together. In the eighteenth century the new science combined with the new political theories of John Locke in the hands of French *philosophes* – learned popularizers of the latest intellectual trends – to produce the Enlightenment. This was essentially a new world view codified as an intellectual movement. It stressed rationality, secularism, and optimism, all of which produced the idea of progress.

This whole set of developments, and Enlightenment views in particular, found expression in historical writing that forms the foundations of modern western historiography. Though not "professional historians" in the sense that nineteenth-century academic historians would come to be, Enlightenment historians included some of the best minds of the age: David Hume, the leading philosopher of the Scottish Enlightenment, was best known in his day for *The History of England, from the invasion of Julius Caesar to the Revolution in 1688*,[24] a multi-volume work that was hugely popular, going through more than 100 editions and remaining the standard history until the mid-nineteenth century. A proponent of Enlightenment universalism, a partisan of neither major political party and a Scot writing English history, Hume's balanced dispassionate judgments often read as more "modern" today than the highly nationalist and often racist histories of the more "scientific" nineteenth century that we will discuss below, despite his access to a more limited range of sources. And even more influential was Edward Gibbon, whose monumental *Decline and Fall of the Roman Empire*[25] is a masterpiece of prose style and for many historians the first "modern" history in its strict reliance on and careful criticism of primary sources. It is still remarkably accurate, characterized by acute judgment, and informed by humane Enlightenment belief in rationality and liberty that led him to link religion and barbarism as the causes of the fall of Rome. None of the great Enlightenment historians focused exclusively on warfare – indeed the same enlightened attitudes led them to view war in a negative moral light – but it formed a significant part of their stories. The century saw continued publication of military memoirs that foreshadowed aspects of later official regimental histories, and the genre of military manuals saw the addition of naval Fighting Instructions that came to have the force of military law.

While historians may not have focused exclusively on military history during the Enlightenment, there was still great interest in military history during the period, often on the part of military men. An early example of one such individual was Raimondo Montecuccoli (1609–80). Montecuccoli saw extensive military service with the Imperial Army, in the Thirty Years War, the Nordic War, the Turkish invasion of Hungary, and the Dutch War of Louis XIV, eventually rising to the rank of Field Marshal in the Imperial Army and President of the Austrian War Council. He wrote several works that circulated in imperial military circles and were apparently viewed as military secrets. Some of his works were later published, and widely distributed in several languages upon his death. His main contribution was to try to extract a set of universal principles of war, setting the stage for later Enlightenment thinkers who sought to find a set of universal principles for the conduct of war.[26]

Interest in military affairs and military history in the eighteenth century is demonstrated by the remarkable increase in the publication of tomes in those areas, especially from the middle of the century onward. During the seventeenth century some 70 works on the military art were published. In the period from 1700 to 1748 another 30 or so appeared, but just in the brief period between the War of the Austrian Succession and the Seven Years War (1748–56) another 25 appeared, and between 1756 and the outbreak of the French Revolution that number quadrupled. Many of the "great captains" of the age, such as Maurice de Saxe and Frederick the Great, wrote histories designed to inform junior officers and other interested parties about the underlying principles of the art of war. Moreover, particularly in France, numerous military officers followed in the footsteps of their commanders, writing works that sought to study military history, especially that of antiquity, in pursuit of understanding the natural laws that governed the conduct of war. One such was Lieutenant Colonel Paul Gideon Joly de Maizeroy who was a leading expert of his time on warfare in the ancient world and who can be credited with drawing the distinction between the realms of the tactics and strategy.[27]

Science, Nationalism and General Staffs: Military History in the Nineteenth and Early Twentieth Centuries

The nineteenth century was a period of rapid and significant change, and the changing historical context contributed to transformations in history writing generally and military history in particular that resulted in the birth of the modern historical profession. Many of the transformations originated in "The West" – Western Europe and its North American off-shoots – and our historiography follows this in focusing on an increasingly Euro-American (and Eurocentric) body of historical writing in this period.

Changing contexts

The French Revolution and the wars of Napoleon, 1789–1815, mark the beginning of the new age. The Revolution (and its American precursor) injected Enlightenment thought into political systems espousing the Rights of Man, the beginning of a process whereby ideology became much more self-conscious. And though Enlightenment principles claimed universal application, the creation of a French Revolutionary army by *levée en masse*, or universal conscription, formed a crucial institutional context for the rise of nationalism as one of the dominant ideologies of the next two centuries. Political and ideological upheaval accompanied military change, as the "limited" wars of maneuver and siege carried out by royal armies that dominated eighteenth-century European conflict gave way to the rapid strategic movements and decisive battles of citizen armies and Napoleonic warfare.

Even more transformative, however, though in some ways less noticed at the time by military theorists, were the effects of the Industrial Revolution. It spawned further political upheaval, creating mass politics that tended to express the class conflict of old aristocracies, bourgeoisie, and proletarians, and of conservatives, liberals, and socialists of various stripes. Mass politics grew from economic transformation based on the mass production and mass consumption of an increasingly middle-class society. Mass readership of mass-produced books and periodicals was an aspect of this, with special relevance to the potential audiences of military history. Technological change was both product and further cause of economic transformation: steam power drove steel production, cloth industries, railroads, and steamships, and armaments industries of unprecedented capacity. New military technologies proliferated, from rifled muskets in 1830 through dreadnought battleships at the turn of the twentieth century to the revolutionary land, sea, and air technologies of the last 100 years. Military organization struggled to keep up with simultaneous changes in technology and sociopolitical context. The problematic relationship between the military, civil society, and political power and stability dominated the thought behind organizational models, of which two competed for primacy. The French model stressed a long service professional army separated from society to make it politically reliable. The Prussian model of universal conscription and reserves went hand-in-hand with mass political education and militarization of society, and dominated continental Europe after its victory over the French in 1870–1. Sea power and distance allowed England and the US to avoid the extremes of this problem for the most part, leading to a less politically charged and more civilian-influenced view of civil–military relationships. The Prussians also pioneered the other crucial aspect of military organization that arose out of the new socioeconomic context: professional general staffs. Mass conscript armies mobilized via a railroad network required detailed professional planning, and general staffs thus became the vital nervous systems of military organizations.

At the same time, the global reach of industrial economics and technology brought western military and political power to new dominance on the global stage and made clear to contemporaries the close link between industrial might and military power. When Marx wrote in *The Communist Manifesto* that "the cheap prices of its commodities is the heavy artillery with which [the bourgeoisie] batter down all Chinese walls," the point is economic, but the military metaphor is telling. Interestingly, however, the technological disparities of much colonial warfare in the period 1870–1945 led European military thinkers to ignore most of that warfare and its potential lessons – what could fights with savages teach Europeans about fighting each other? Even the American Civil War received little attention outside the US after its conclusion, although interest in it revived, at least in Britain, after World War I.

Of the many ideologies birthed in this context, three had particular influence on the writing of history, especially military history. We have mentioned nationalism already. Nationalism is the conscious promotion of "national" identity over all other forms of communal identity. Since "nations" – theoretically, a people sharing a common language, culture, racial characteristics (in nineteenth-century thought), and, crucially, history – are, unlike states or economies, artificial constructs, the role of historians (professional or not) in creating a sense of a shared past assumed a prominent place in modern societies analogically equivalent to the role of royal court historians in the traditional world. The stakes of history writing went up, in other words, and history writing became trapped in the confines of political borders in ways that it is only very recently beginning to escape. But transcending national boundaries in shaping historical writing were the idea of progress and the influence of romanticism. European dominance in the world of the nineteenth century fits well with linear views of history as a story of constant improvement technologically and morally, and unlike Christian or Marxist linear views, which both had utopian endpoints, the Victorian notion of progress was theoretically unlimited (and of course could have national leaders). The complex of ideas known as romanticism do not admit of a simple definition, but contributed heavily to notions of idealized tribal pasts that lay at the root of much European nationalist historiography, as well as informing notions of "natural genius" that allowed brilliant generalship to be equated with artistic or scientific genius. Caesar would have been pleased.

Military history, 1800–1918.

Given the sheer military impact of the Napoleonic Wars, it is not surprising that the most significant military writing to appear in their immediate aftermath was not history (though many histories were, of course, written) but theoretical analyses. The two most important writers were Antoine Henri Jomini, a Swiss soldier who served both in and against Napoleon's armies, and Carl von Clausewitz, a Prussian officer who fought against Napoleon.[28] Though today Clausewitz is far better known (especially outside military circles) and has been more influential, both contributed significantly to modern military analysis. Both emphasized the importance of superior numbers in war. But Jomini emphasized secure bases and lines of operation, the capture of key strategic points, and a preference for speed and maneuver over pitched battle, whereas Clausewitz emphasized concentration of force for a decisive battle of annihilation. (Some historians see less difference between the two, claiming that emphasizing maneuver over battle misreads Jomini.) Clausewitz also stressed the role of "friction" – the accumulation of unexpected, unpredictable and unknowable impediments to the smooth functioning of military plans – in the conduct of war, in a romantically inspired but very realistic reaction against what he saw as the excessive rationalism of Enlightenment theorists who had tried to formulate pseudo-mathematical laws of war. Clausewitz stressed instead close attention to historical case studies that illustrated both general principles but also the uniqueness of each situation and the effects of friction. At the end of the century, Alfred Thayer Mahan and Julian Corbett, inspired by Jomini and Clausewitz respectively, developed the intellectual framework for modern naval theory and making naval strategy an integral part of national military strategy.[29] Mahan was, like Clausewitz, historically oriented methodologically, as he developed his principles through a close study of eighteenth-century and Napoleonic naval warfare.

These theoretical studies were, however, increasingly seen as something separate from military history as such. This is because professionalization in two distinct but related forms was the dominant theme in the nineteenth century for military history. The first form that this took grew out of the emergence of the Prussian general staff system. The careful, detailed, and meticulous planning of rail-based mobilizations and maneuvers that necessitated general staffs created an intellectual environment conducive to the equally careful and theoretically informed study of the history of war aimed at extracting strategic lessons for planning future wars. Staff studies of potential theaters led to staff studies of past campaigns, which led on to official histories of campaigns conducted by the staff. Official historians had access to all the official material – planning documents, dispatches, reports from the front – generated during the course of a campaign, and wrote with an eye to learning how to improve military performance the next time. At times, as in the case of Helmuth von Moltke the Elder, who led the Prussian army in the Franco-Prussian War, historian and general were the same man. But this was on a very different, academically trained model from the general's-eye-view war reporting of Caesar.

For the other face of professionalization was the academic. History, not just military but all history, became a specialized, professional field of an increasingly professionalized academia in the mid-nineteenth century. The training ground was the seminar; the principle was close attention to primary sources critically assessed that would allow the historian to create an objective picture of the past "as it actually happened"; and the father figure who created this new system of training was Leopold von Ranke. Historians trained in von Ranke's seminars at Berlin University, or in similar settings created in imitation of von Ranke's system in England, France, and the United States, came to constitute a separate class of academically prestigious historians who wrote not only books but also specialist articles published in newly created professional historical journals such as *Historische Zeitschrift*, *The English Historical Review*, and *The American Historical Review*, all of which continue to exist to this day as the flagship publications of their national academic communities of historians.

Though largely separate phenomena (since military history constituted only a small fraction of academic historians, whose focus was mostly political, institutional, and religious history), these two sorts of professional historian could meet in one person, the most famous and influential example being Hans Delbrück. Delbrück was a student of a von Ranke student, taught at Berlin, and also had connections to the German General Staff. Delbrück's critical attention to sources tested against physical possibility through the use of economics and demography revolutionized the study of ancient and medieval warfare, and he situated the history of war in the broader flow of historical development: the English title of his major work is *The History of Warfare in the Framework of Political History*,[30] and accurately reflects his concern to relate modes of military organization and practice to social and political structures. He was therefore situated to be the father of modern military history. But, especially in the Anglo-American world, he wasn't.[31]

This is in part because his focus on the links between military history and politics highlighted a certain Prussian militarism that fit poorly with more civilian Anglo-American ideals. It was partly because both German and French military history after 1870, and even more after 1918, was such a loaded subject that it generated narrow, parochial historiographies that could not even pretend to approach the unrealizable ideal of von Rankean objectivity. But it was partly because the tradition of Anglo-American military historiography, especially with regard to battle histories, had already been set in 1851 by Sir Edward Creasy's *Fifteen Decisive Battles of the World*.[32] Creasy, an amateur historian who taught briefly at Oxford, managed to combine a powerfully attractive mixture of historiographical traditions in one simple recipe. The key was the notion of "decisiveness," which removed the taint of moral suspicion that interest in battle details held for Victorian sensibilities by linking the results of battles to the notion of progress, or in specifically English terms to the Whig interpretation of history. It could thus legitimize the narrative thrills of the Caesarian "battle piece" by providing it with a moral. The "world" (really the western world) frame allowed a broad, inclusive, and apparently objective view of military history that extended back to the Greeks, whose defeat of the Persians at Marathon became the opening victory in the battle between freedom and oriental despotism, without precluding a nationalist slant available via the selection of battles (Creasy's last battle was Waterloo). It therefore could also marry the popular and academic strands of military history, as well as attracting practitioners from the ranks of retired military men. The book went through many editions, inspired libraries-full of imitators and continuators,[33] and overshadowed for a century any other major approach to military history – the circulation of other academic and official histories was miniscule by comparison. In popular historiography it still exercises a significant influence.[34]

Taken as a whole, military historiography produced by increasingly professionalized academic historians and military staffs in the nineteenth and early twentieth centuries can be seen as developing two major characteristics. The first, based in its theoretical roots in Clausewitz and others, as well as the generalship tradition embedded in the Caesarian battle narrative (Decisive Battles, after all, are won by Great Men), was a focus on the art of war as its central topic. Analyses of campaigns and battles sought examples of universal military principles, not the fine grain of historical context and difference that leads to an understanding of past events on their own terms. Delbrück's linking of military and social structures lost out even in medieval history, at least in the English-speaking world, to Charles Oman's *Art of War in the Middle Ages*,[35] originally an 1888 undergraduate prize essay whose active shelf life extended well into the 1970s and beyond. One result was that military history became increasingly distant from other fields of academic history, especially those influenced by the economic and social analyses of Karl Marx.

The other characteristic (or related set of characteristics), on the other hand, is common to most nineteenth-century history: it was nationalist, racist, and Eurocentric. The common frame for the "decisiveness" of battles (or for the development of political institutions in the Delbrückian mode) was the modern nation-state: battles were significant for the degree to which they contributed to the emergence of the Great Powers of nineteenth-century Europe and the US. And the results of battles and national development were not a story of chance and opportunistic politics, but expressions of essentialized national characters: Hasting in 1066 as a clash between Norman aristocratic tyranny (or virtue) and freedom-loving, proto-democratic (or degenerate) Anglo-Saxons[36] is merely a particularly clear example of a near-universal outlook. Finally, from this perspective, war beyond Europe hardly mattered, even if it involved Europeans. Chinese military history and its long historiography might never have existed, and potentially valuable lessons from the Crimean War, the American Civil War, and the Boer War went largely unanalyzed and unappreciated – Frederick the Great's campaigns remained a more popular subject for analysis in 1900 than the contemporary experiences of the British in South Africa. It was this historiographical tradition, along with the rest of the world of the nineteenth century, that was confronted with the ugly facts of 1914–45.

New Military Histories: The Transformations of the Last 50 Years

If nothing replaced the nineteenth-century paradigm for military history in the immediate aftermath of World War I (and indeed, for some time after World War II), it was in part because academic military history went into eclipse in the wake of those wars. Military history in the Creasy tradition continued to find a popular audience, and official histories, operational histories of campaigns and battles, continued to be written. These included the excellent and methodologically sophisticated official US histories of World War II – the "Green Series" – under the direction of S. E. Morison, and studies by S. L. A. Marshall in *Infantry* magazine that carefully investigated the actual experience of battle of individual soldiers. These found an academic counterpart in Bell I. Wiley's pioneering social histories of military life in the American Civil War, *The Life of Johnny Reb* and *The Life of Billy Yank*, published during and just after World War II.[37] And indeed a number of important academic histories of war and warfare were published during this era, many focused on World War I.[38] But for the most part academic military history was the province of a small minority who found little respect in academia generally, and the three sorts of military history – popular, professional, and academic – became more separate. It is necessary to understand this period of eclipse to understand the trajectory of military history in the last 50 years.

Academic eclipse, 1918–58

The effect of the wars themselves was partly responsible for this. Pacifism, anti-militarism, and socialist and populist

ideologies antithetical to the outlook of the contemporary
military history tradition gained in popularity everywhere,
including in the British and US academic community. The
results of World War II kept military history as a fraught
topic for German and French intellectuals. The Cold War and
McCarthyism further alienated US academics from a form of
history that could too easily be read as supportive of or contributing to the growth of military industrial complexes and
the erosion of civilian values at the expense of militarism.

But the academy in the 1950s, even more than today, was
by no means monolithically leftist, and in the US was in fact
largely conservative. So other factors necessarily played a role
in military history's going so thoroughly out of favor. The
continued vitality of the popular market for military history
ironically played some role here, as it fostered lots of historical writing of questionable quality. The bad reputation this
fostered, plus a bit of academic snobbery, conspired to limit
the impact even of good popular histories and of official
histories. The continued advance of specialization and professionalization furthermore reinforced this attitude by
making popularity itself suspect: real academic history was
aimed at other academics. Finally, military history came up
short in competition with other more traditional, prestigious
sorts of history – political, institutional, and religious history
still dominated academic publishing – and with economic
history, Marxist and otherwise, that resonated with recent
experiences of Depression and a war won by industrial
might. It would take a new generation of academics from different backgrounds to begin the process of reviving academic
military history.

War and society, 1958–88

There was no little amount of irony in the academic reaction
against military history, since the impact of both world wars
could be read as clear proof of the importance of war in history, not just in political and economic terms, but in terms of
catalyzing social change (the American Civil Rights movement
and the rise of women's labor are only two examples) and
as a shaper of popular culture (the instant and enduring

popularity of World War II and the Nazis in popular history, movies, and TV being the obvious case, as well as the enduring interest in the US Civil War). But two related developments in the demographics of American graduate study reinforced the academic prejudice against military history. First, the early 1960s saw an influx into graduate history programs of a much broader range of students in terms of ethnicity, class, and gender – ironically again, many the beneficiaries of the educational assistance of the US GI Bill, which paid the college expenses of US veterans. Their interests lay largely in bringing the neglected voices of their pasts to history, which mostly meant a focus on aspects of social history. They also tended to bring a more liberal political perspective to the professoriate. At the same time, the Vietnam War both confirmed that liberalism and contributed to turning it against war – indeed some entered academia in part to avoid the draft. In that context, studying warfare became associated with glorifying it, or at least supporting it. Nor was this a nonsensical stance, for the "battle piece" narrative tradition that stretched from Herodotus and Caesar through Creasy continued to inform popular military history, and it always contained a strong element of glorifying war and great commanders, often at the expense of understanding what the experience of war was like for individual soldiers. A generation that mistrusted authority and protested the war its country was fighting was justifiably unlikely to buy into that historiographical tradition. Yet among old and new academics alike, the importance of warfare in history could not be totally ignored. And the inclination toward social history that emerged at this time in the historical profession as a whole turned out to create a pathway for military history to re-enter the academy through a new door: war and society studies.

In summary form, what war and society historians began to do was redefine military history away from an exclusive focus on the art of war – away, that is, from just studying campaigns and battles as exemplars of universal military principles. Instead, they began to focus on the impact of warfare, including preparations for making war and institutional arrangements for supporting military forces, on society more broadly. As this impact was often (though not exclusively) negative, war and society studies could find some acceptance across the political spectrum. Studying the impact of war on society also led to studies of the impact of society (social organization, mechanisms of informal power, economic systems) on how warfare was organized and fought. Professional Military Education, which increasingly viewed the art of war not as a matter of individual genius but as a product of institutional processes, contributed to a climate open to war and society studies. In studying both sides of this reciprocal relationship, the conceptual and methodological tools historians had begun to develop for doing social history generally proved useful, and the ultimate focus of such studies on the impact of war rather than on war itself allowed those doing such history to call themselves social or institutional historians (whose topic happened to touch on war) and so make themselves more employable in the eyes of history departments making new hires.

In terms of making war and society studies academically acceptable, it is also probably not insignificant that some of the groundbreaking works looked at medieval societies. This was partly because medieval Europe was, in various ways, a society dominated by a warrior aristocracy and organized for making war, so that the importance of the topic needed little defending, and furthermore could claim, from a nationalist perspective, the origins in organizing for war of many of the modern institutions of state and governance. And it was partly that medieval times were nevertheless distant and different enough to mute the potentially contentious political implications of such studies. H. J. Hewitt's *The Organization of War under Edward III* (1958) and Warren Hollister's *Anglo-Saxon Military Institutions on the Eve of the Norman Conquest* (1962) and *The Military Organization of Norman England* (1964) demonstrated the potential of the institutional side of this approach, while R. C. Smail's brilliant *Crusading Warfare, 1097–1193* (1959)[39] showed that institutional and social studies of warfare could also make significant contributions to understanding "art of war" questions, as he demonstrated that the standard battle-avoiding patterns of medieval warfare, often condemned from a Clausewitzian perspective as ranging from indecisive to ignorantly incompetent, in fact made sense against the background of Crusader state manpower restrictions and social arrangements. But generally, a common characteristic of war and society studies, especially of the Hewitt–Hollister sort, is that they tended to take the actual conduct of war out of military history. Armies were recruited, organized, fed, paid, and sent home; they sometimes marched, but they never fought. Military institutions also look clearer and more organized in peacetime, leading institutional studies away from war itself. But ultimately, fighting is what armies must be designed to do, even if they do so rarely, and the test of military systems comes during war, so despite wide acceptance, such studies left some military historians dissatisfied.

Follow-ups to these leads in medieval history and beyond remained relatively rare until at least the mid-1970s, and it was only in the early 1980s that war and society studies began to appear in significant numbers and gained recognition under the rubric "The New Military History" (which by now is no longer so new). This reflects both inertia in the political climate of academia – the bad reputation of military history died hard (and isn't completely dead yet) – and the slow pace of generational change as PhDs took longer to complete and graduates took longer to find jobs in a job market that was very sluggish through much of the 1980s. But military history received further impetus toward academic respectability with the publication in 1976 of John Keegan's *The Face of Battle*.[40] It is hard to overstate the importance of this book to the development of the field. Keegan's study of common soldiers' experience of the battlefield consciously attempted to redefine the military history of combat away from the Creasy paradigm. Its introduction spelled out the historiographical problem; three case studies widely separated in time brought not just a social historian's sensibility but also a psychological insight to the evidence; and the conclusion placed this study of war by a professor at Sandhurst, the British military academy, firmly in an anti-war frame. It blazed a path into war and society studies for the study of actual warfare, inspiring enough similar studies that "face of battle" history has become a type within modern military history. And it managed to unite important strands from official histories (especially the US official histories of World War II noted above) and academic history into a package that bridged the academic–popular divide. "The New Military History" that blossomed in the early 1980s thus flowed from the pairing of war and society and face of battle studies.

New paths, since 1988

Though "The New Military History" was gaining in influence by the late 1980s, its impact on academic history more broadly remained somewhat limited. Its visibility has broadened since 1988 thanks to the publication of another very important book, Geoffrey Parker's *The Military Revolution. Military Innovation and the Rise of the West, 1500–1800.*[41] That military history had advanced a long way already is indicated by the fact that Parker was building on an idea first proposed by Michael Roberts in 1955.[42] Roberts's "military revolution" had been largely ignored outside military history circles and some specialist literature on the early modern state. Parker's book had immediate and widespread influence.

The main reason for this is that Parker put military change at the heart of an explanation for two phenomena that had, and continue to have, wide currency in history generally: the genesis of the modern state; and the origins of western dominance globally since 1800, with implications for widespread arguments about western exceptionalism. We will examine the details of this argument and the controversies surrounding it more closely in chapter 4. What is important to understand here is that whether non-military historians agreed with Parker or not, they had to deal with his sophisticated and wide-ranging argument, and as a result military history entered into the mainstream of discussion about the causes of phenomena that all historians accepted as significant. Within military history, Parker's work furthermore stimulated an ongoing debate about the concept of "military revolutions" generally, which we will also examine further in chapter 4. Finally, the sorts of issues Parker raised pointed military history toward two trends that have become increasingly important in the historiography of the last fifteen years. The first, the increasing influence of global perspectives and world historical approaches, arose naturally out of the global claims of Parker's thesis and the comparisons, implicit and explicit, he drew between military systems. The second was there more by implication, but was nonetheless clear: that culture was an important factor in shaping military practice. Cultural analysis and the theoretical insights developed for thinking about culture by other branches of history have thus become part of the historiography of military history, tying it more closely to mainstream historiography.

Both these trends have had implications not just for the topics and methods of military history but also for the range of its practitioners. If serious military history had contracted by the early twentieth century to a field studied in the Anglo-American world and, more problematically, in Germany and France, it is now an increasingly global concern in terms of writers and audiences as well as topic. Chinese and Japanese military history in particular have grown recently, coinciding with the renewed popularity of Sunzi's *Art of War* not only as a source for military history and theory but as a guide to business strategy (a use also imposed at times on Clausewitz).

The (no longer so new) military history with its foundations in social history continues to flourish alongside these more recent approaches based in global and cultural perspectives, even if all the practitioners of military history still constitute a small minority of professional academic historians. It is a sign of the vitality of military history that new approaches continue to emerge. We shall look at the recent conceptual and theoretical trends outlined above in more detail in chapter 3, and examine some of the current debates and controversies affecting the field in chapter 4. These trends in academic history have also affected both the publication industry that is popular military history (including new venues such as television) and the contours of Professional Military Education, as academics have moved from ignoring these branches of military history to colonizing them. The lines separating academic, popular, and professional military are blurring, in other words, recreating in some ways the dynamics of the less specialized military literatures of ancient and medieval times, but reconstructed around the standards and methods of professional academic historians. Meanwhile, the globalizing pool of military historians and their audiences is recreating the range and diversity that military writing had in ancient times. For military historians and their audiences, this can only be a good thing.

3

Conceptual Frameworks

As a broad, growing, and contested field, military history is practiced by historians with a wide range of philosophical and methodological perspectives. But the conceptual core of military history lies at the intersection of specifically military concepts with ideas and methods increasingly common to many areas of contemporary historical inquiry. This chapter surveys the conceptual frameworks that inform military history, moving from specifically military concepts to new modes of inquiry. First, however, the historiography of military history surveyed in chapter 2 raises some basic questions about the philosophy of military history, that is about the basic assumptions military historians make in studying military history. Military historians, perhaps because of the self-professed practicality of much their work for military professionals and trainees, have by and large been slower than those in many historical fields to engage in critical examination of their assumptions. We will look at how military history has generally handled two fundamental questions about history: how do we explain the past (what is our theory of causation); and how do we understand the past (what is our theory of access to historical mentalities).

Military History and Philosophy of History

Causation

The more obvious philosophical aspect of military history focuses on the issue of causation. Military historians' traditional philosophical stance on this issue from the time of earliest royal propaganda has tended toward what most historians today refer to, disparagingly, as Great Man history. That is, military history has studied the victories (and sometimes the heroic defeats) of successful and glorious leaders – kings and generals – under the assumption that those victories were important not just in themselves, but for the wider course of history. The natural product of this view of historical causation is the tradition in western military historiography of the "Decisive Battles" books discussed in chapter 2. "Decisive Battles" were decisive, in this view, not in producing a one-sided victory but in changing the course of history, and the outcome of the battle is assumed to originate in the skillful generalship of the winning side's commander. Thus, great military leaders change the course of history and qualify as "great men," historiographically.

Great Man history has not been universal in earlier military history. Neither Herodotus nor Thucydides subscribed to such a view, and for much of the Middle Ages the ultimate cause of victory in battle, and indeed the ultimate cause of anything significant, was seen to be God's will, which potentially reduced somewhat the credit successful leaders could claim directly. But the medieval view still often focused on the leader. And "Greatness" need not have a single definition, of course: different cultures have valued different qualities in their leaders. Medieval "great men" were those favored by God, and were furthermore those who showed great bravery and daring. Chinese leaders, in the historiographical tradition of Sunzi and later Confucianism, on the other hand, were supposed to display intelligence, control, and mastery of written principles of war. But whether through intelligence or bravery, leaders in this view controlled battles and battles controlled history.

The assumptions underlying such a view have come under

increasing question in the last century among academic historians, though in both popular history (because biography and Top Ten lists are favorites of the reading public) and to a lesser extent in professional military education (where the assumption that leadership matters gains a certain force of necessity) Great Man history in one form or another remains common. What influence do most individuals really have on history? Can they even control battles the way a chess player can control his "army"? (We will discuss the notions of "friction" and the "fog of war" further below.) Furthermore, the criteria for "decisiveness" in evaluating battles are by no means straightforward, and careful evaluation of the long-term effect of most battles probably shows that they made little deep impact.[1] As a result, other views of causation than Great Man have gained ground in military history, a trend shared with all fields of history in recent decades.

At the other end of the scale of causation from Great Men and Decisive Battles stands a view narrated very effectively by Leo Tolstoy in his novel *War and Peace.* Though not a history but a novel, *War and Peace* still consciously lays out a philosophical perspective on causation in history generally and warfare in particular, with the battle of Borodino forming Tolstoy's "case study." In this view, the actions of leaders are virtually irrelevant to the course of a battle. The complexity of events, their impossibility of being controlled, and the multiple paths they could have taken mean that all of history is simply contingent: one path among many possible ones through time, with the differences separating possible paths down almost entirely to chance. This does not make the events of history random; paths of causation can be traced backwards. Contingent history is explicable but not predictable; contingency cautions not only against attributing too much influence to leaders but also implies that the lessons or principles of successful leadership one might gain from studying their careers are likely to be illusory.

The rise of social history in the last 50 years has contributed, paradoxically, to undermining both Great Man history and strict contingency. Whether in the form of *Annales* school history in France, whose philosophical assumptions were explicit from the beginning, or in the more diffuse theory and practice of Anglo-American social history,

the emphasis of social history on long-term processes, demographics, the historical experiences and agency of common
people, and deep constraints imposed by environment and
modes of production has contributed strongly to downgrading
the role of individual leaders in creating historical change. Yet
at the same time, those same characteristics seem to show
that many separate contingent paths of historical experience
can fall into patterns and are subject to the deep constraints
social history has exposed. It was not until the rise of "war
and society" studies (see chapter 2) that social historical outlooks on causation made significant inroads into military
history – the influence of Marxism on military history has
been almost exclusively indirect, via social history and analysis of social structures and how they shaped military
organization, for instance, though Marxist analysis had
transformed economic and much social history far earlier.

The question of causation in military history has long been
influenced, however, by a particular view of structural constraints that stresses the role of technology in shaping patterns
of warfare. This emphasis is not surprising, given the prominent and visible role weaponry plays in how wars are fought,
especially in our modern world of rapid technological change.
The looming threat of global nuclear destruction in the Cold
War era gave military technology special prominence.[2] But
too often the very visibility and "gee whiz" attractiveness of
military technology has led military historians to overempha-
size technology at the expense of other explanatory factors, a
view in its extreme form known as Technological Determinism
from its tendency to ascribe all significant change to changes
in technology. The oversimplification involved in Technological
Determinist views of military history is regularly exposed by
more nuanced studies that show how deeply the use of technology is shaped by social and cultural factors that vary
widely over different societies. Thus, social historical
approaches have undermined Technological Determinism as
much as they have Great Man history.

In short, the analysis of the structures and constraints of
long-term historical trends has prompted military historians
to see causation as both more deeply embedded in those
structures and constraints – the greater recognition of the
importance of logistics in shaping strategy has been one clear

result in recent military history of this trend – and more broadly spread out than either Great Man history or technological determinism claims, yet probably less totally open and undirected than Tolstoyan contingency implies. Complex contingent paths, perhaps influenced by moments of great military leadership or decisive warfare among a multitude of causal factors, exist in this view within boundaries whose shape changes only slowly and gradually. But how do those boundaries or structures change?

Recently, cultural theory has contributed to the question of causation and how change happens and has offered a theoretical approach to the intersection of individual action and cultural change over time. But to see how that branch of historical theory applies to military history, it is necessary first to explore the other major philosophical problem in military history, a problem that revolves around views of human nature and its relevance to military history.

Military minds

The most common and often historiographically dominant approach to military history in modern developed countries has been the one influenced by professional military education. The major theme of this approach, as we saw in chapter 2, has been a search for "universal military principles" of strategy and tactics. Put another way, this approach mines the past for lessons about the "art of warfare" – that this is the title of Sunzi's classical Chinese book on war indicates the ancient and cross-cultural credentials of this approach. Yet Sunzi was mining a specifically Chinese and, for him, not so ancient past for examples of good military practice. Extending this approach to global millennia raises some interesting questions about how we understand what past military practitioners were up to.[3]

The fundamental assumption behind art of war studies is that universal military principles are founded on universal military thought. This in turn rests on a "rational" model of the past, that is, a model that sees rationality as something common to human analysis of military (or other intellectual) challenges and assumes that rational analysis will therefore produce similar results in similar situations through time and across cultures. Assumptions about a rational past usually include a "rational man" model of military leadership, meaning that military decisions that look sound from a modern rationalist perspective must have been made by rational leaders. The corollary, of course, is that military behavior that seems incomprehensible from a rationalist perspective must have been either badly thought out (and perhaps reached on the basis of incomplete information) or, in fact, irrational and senseless. The rationalist assumption therefore conveys the apparent benefit of creating a universal scale for judging the quality of military leadership. Assumptions about a rational past also usually include a "rational organization" theory of military institutions. Although the influence of social structures and cultural beliefs on military organization has in general been more readily recognized than their influence on individual decision-making, the underlying belief of rationalist assumptions about organizations is that questions of military efficiency will ultimately win out, in a sort of Darwinian process, over social and cultural inefficiencies within a society, or that societies and states that disappear as a result of loss in warfare suffered the consequences of the irrationality of their military organization.

The rationality of rationalist assumptions also tends to be largely materialist. At the level of source criticism this leads to the principle that Hans Delbrück called *Sachkritik*, or measuring what ancient sources have to say against the limits of physical possibility. While useful for debunking extreme claims, especially about numbers of troops (e.g. Herodotus' claim that Darius marched more than a million men across the Hellespont in his invasion of Greece in 481 BCE), it is of limited utility in any case where physical reality admits of multiple possibilities, which is most of the time.[4] More problematic is the assumption of materialist rationality that underlies views of military and political goals, views that include the principle of *Realpolitik* that sees warfare and politics aimed at concrete material goals and that can include the Clausewitzian dictum that "war is merely the continuation of policy by other means." A final related assumption often linked to these through the assumed rationality of politics, though not necessarily a direct result of rationalist models, is that "states" are the proper level of political unit for military analysis.

The universal rationalist model has often led to military history that ignores social and cultural factors, separating the military art and military organization from its historical context in order to make clearer the supposed universal principles and lessons. Even the much more nuanced and social history-influenced approach to "face of battle" studies initiated by Keegan's *Face of Battle* (see chapter 2) makes a weaker universalist claim: that basic human emotions are similar across both time and culture and therefore accessible and comprehensible to the modern historian. This claim too can separate the experiences of historical actors from the contexts and cultural norms that gave meaning to their decisions at the time.

This is not to say that such assumptions are always wrong. What has often been deeply problematic in military history is that these assumptions, even when defensible, have not been made explicit and have therefore not been defended. For they raise a number of questions that military historians have only recently begun to grapple with in any depth. Are there, for instance, cultural influences on rationality, and on political and military goals, that if uncovered can make sense of apparently irrational behavior? Is there indeed one universal standard of rationality? Along another line, access to past minds may not always be transparent. Are emotions truly universal, or do cultural contexts and practices influence both their expression and their meaning? Finally, postmodernist questions about the meaning and use of language – the key insights of deconstructionism – raise serious questions about the meaning(s) of sources. Military terminology itself, including such apparently straightforward terms as "infantry" and "cavalry," may have different meanings over time and across cultures that affect, especially in translations of sources, how we see the organization and motivation of military action and organization.[5]

Many contemporary military historians have begun to examine these universalist assumptions, and an alternative view that places military decisions and systems in their social and cultural context, and then tries to assess them in their own historicized terms, has emerged. This social constructionist view gained ground initially in "war and society" studies whose focus was on social impacts and meanings, but has since spread to studies of military organizations and cultures in their own right.

The constructionist view may make cross-cultural comparisons of generalship – defined as adherence to art of war principles – more difficult, but trades that loss for greater insight into how military leaders saw the military and political problems they faced. It does not claim that past military leaders were irrational, but it does attempt to show that rationality, and what can count as a rational goal, need not conform to our own modern preconceptions, especially materialist ones. Religious precepts and cultural conventions about the meaning of battle (that, for instance, battle was an essentially judicial procedure whose outcome was in God's hands and that it therefore should be sought when "rational" analysis might suggest that avoiding it would be a safer alternative, a common view in early medieval European warfare) might have dictated courses of action to past military leaders that violated supposedly universal principles of generalship. Such instances from a universalist perspective may look merely pointless; from a constructionist perspective they are comprehensible, even if they carry few lessons about the military art for modern commanders. Institutional models and emotional reactions to battle can also be better understood using this approach. And careful attention to the context of warfare can also undermine the state-centered assumptions underlying much rationalist history by historicizing states and their ideologies (especially modern ideologies, nationalism above all) and highlighting non-state actors and cultural parameters of warfare. In this case, not only does a less state-centered view of warfare make better sense of patterns of aristocratic violence in many pre-modern societies and bring peoples to the historical stage, including nomadic tribes, previously neglected in military historical study, but it has the additional benefit of offering potentially better "lessons" for modern policy makers faced with conflict against non-traditional enemies including terrorists and guerilla insurgencies.

The constructionist view has advanced in military historiography hand-in-hand with more structuralist views of causation. But structuralist views applied to analysis of individual actions can run the danger of reading too much constraint into social and cultural norms and so making change over time difficult to explain. In other words, if all individual actions are determined by the structural constraints imposed by social and cultural norms, and those norms are so widely and deeply embedded as to be immutable, then how do the undeniable differences between societies in different eras arise? One possible answer is obvious: when radically different cultural (and/or military) systems meet, radical change may be forced on some and likely all of the systems involved. The Spanish encounter with the Aztecs certainly challenged Mesoamerican cultural and social norms of warfare; the resulting conquest left neither side unchanged. But most change is neither so radical nor so catastrophic, even in military history – as noted above, very few battles are truly decisive to the extent of changing the deep structures of historical possibility. Given this, what generates what we might call "everyday change"?

Here we return to the recent cultural theory, much of it French in origin, mentioned above. Reduced to its basics, such theory sounds commonsensical. No historical construct – society, culture or political system – is static. The apparent boundaries are constantly created, recreated, and (usually) reinforced by individuals' performance of social roles and cultural beliefs. But this very performative character of individual action means that at the margins, performance can question, subvert, and even alter the accepted boundaries of behavior. The changes thus produced need not be dramatic or swift; indeed, the broadly social nature of the process mostly ensures that it will not be. But the process this theory models does leave room for the contingent paths of individual historical actors, including military actors at all levels, not just Great Men, to exert transformative pressure on the boundaries of their cultural worlds, and not to be merely constrained by them.

The very act of theorizing about forces of change and modeling cultural behavior still strikes many practitioners and readers of military history as somehow unnecessary. But, as is true in any field of history, and as much military history has demonstrated to its detriment, all history is based on assumptions, theories, and models. The historiographical lesson is that the assumptions, theories, and models that are taken most for granted and are thus least examined are the very ones that can be most misleading. Spotting assumptions and being critical about underlying theory is often the first task of the intelligent student of military history.

Military Art and Practice

Although military history has been particularly prone to being framed in terms of Great Man or Technological Determinist theories of causation and in terms of its own peculiar universalisms, the philosophical questions outlined above apply in one way or another to all fields of history, and in fact change has come to military history largely through the influence of other schools of historical research. There are, however, concepts specifically generated by military history itself. While military historians' understanding of these concepts and their applicability (universal or otherwise) has in some cases been affected by the philosophical debates outlined in the previous section and the new methodological influences discussed in the following section, their centrality to the study of military history requires explanation of them in their own terms.

Levels of military action and analysis

Probably the most fundamental set of terms relating to the history of military activity are those that specify the level of action being described. The two most common ones, "strategy" and "tactics," are in common use outside military circles and have acquired broad and indeed significantly overlapping meanings that can be seriously confusing when analysis of armed conflict enters the picture. This section attempts to define these key terms, although even in military analysis there is some overlap and fuzziness of boundaries between the levels described. We will move from lowest to highest.

Armed combat starts at the individual level, and this is where *tactics* begin. Tactics are the techniques used by individuals to bring their weapons to bear against other individuals in hand-to-hand combat; the word also describes how small groups of soldiers work together on the battlefield to perform a task (or a mission, in military terms) and how various small groups interact with other groups in their own force and against groups in the enemy force. In other words, tactics are what armed forces use in combat. They can be offensive (a cavalry charge, a tank attack, etc.) or defensive (a shield wall, digging a trench, or occupying a fortification, among other tactics). Since weapons can include ships and airplanes and the weapons those can carry, tactics can also apply to ship-to-ship combat and larger fleet battles and air-to-air combat (dog-fighting) and larger air battles, for example, the Battle of Britain between the Royal Air Force and the Luftwaffe in World War II. (Technically, ships and planes are *weapons* only when the ship or plane itself inflicts damage on the enemy, as with oared warships with rams or kamikaze planes. They more commonly act as *weapons platforms*. The combination of weapons that a platform or force deploys is its *weapons system*.) Interaction of different sorts of weapons in battle is also tactical: tactical air cover is provided by friendly aircraft attacking enemy ground or naval forces and defending friendly ground or naval forces from air attack.

The management of an entire battle is also a tactical matter, and generals direct the tactical deployment of troops, maintain tactical reserves on the battlefield, and are said to seize the tactical initiative by attacking or otherwise forcing the action in a battle. But the deployments and orders directing a large army in an extended battle shade up into a somewhat ambiguous level usually called *grand tactics*. The grand tactical level thus refers to the direction of a battle as a whole, sometimes in terms of a predetermined plan by which a battle unfolds. In modern warfare involving huge armies spread over battlefields hundreds of miles across and deep and involved in battles lasting sometimes weeks or even months, grand tactics become an important aspect of *operations*. The operational level of warfare refers to the management of campaigns and specific theaters of a war, and in large modern wars campaigns and battles can converge toward identity: the Battle of the Bulge was both an operational stroke by the German army and a resulting grand tactical conflict played out between the German and American forces. But in warfare before rifled muskets and railroads (roughly the 1830s), and in some more recent conflicts, it is useful to distinguish the two levels. Pre-modern armies were smaller and moved more slowly than modern armed forces; weapons had much more limited ranges, and therefore the distinction between maneuvering – i.e. marching – through the countryside before meeting the enemy army (generally considered an aspect of operations) and deploying for battle with the enemy in sight (grand tactical deployment) was both clearer than in modern war and reflected in the different formations armies often used for the two stages (columns for marching and lines or squares or other formations for battle). Operations describes the maneuvering stage, the techniques, ruses, marches, and feigned marches that could aim variously at bringing the enemy army to battle in favorable circumstances, or at avoiding battle altogether. Only when battle loomed did grand tactical maneuvering and deployment commence. At the other side of the scale, the tactics used by individual units are usefully distinguished from the grand tactical battle plans generals tried to implement.

Operations can also be seen as the specific implementation of *strategy*. Strategy is the level of military action and analysis that has to do with deciding the objectives of operations in specific theaters, taking into account factors that influence the planning of those operations in pursuit of the overall political objective. Simply put, strategy is the plan for winning a war as opposed to a battle or campaign. It is usefully contrasted not just with operations, for which strategy establishes the overall goals and military rationale, but at the highest level with *grand strategy*. Grand strategy is where warfare and politics merge: a country's grand strategy in a war describes its goals not in strictly military terms but in political, economic, or even cultural terms with military action, including strategy, seen from this perspective as one tool, with diplomacy, bribery, marriage alliance, and so forth, of grand strategy. As a result of its breadth and multifaceted nature, a polity's grand strategy can be more or less explicit, more or less intentional, and sometimes very long term, applying not just to specific wars but to all international relations – rarely are grand strategies as clearly formulated and limited in application as was the Allies' grand strategy for World War II. A grand strategy can thus be subject to significant disagreement among historians about what it was and whether it even existed (coherent grand strategy not being a necessity for the waging of war).[6]

An example can illustrate these somewhat abstract categories a bit more clearly. Let us take Napoleon's famous Austerlitz campaign of 1805 as that example. Napoleon's grand strategy was somewhat in flux at the beginning of the campaign: while his main objective, defeating Britain and thereby ensuring the security of the French Empire from its most dangerous enemy, was constant. British naval superiority had removed any hope that it could be accomplished by direct invasion of the island and made the strategic deployment of the Grande Armée along the Channel coast otiose. But the renewal of war with Sweden, Russia, and Austria at least gave him a strategic objective from which a new grand strategy (aside from beating these three continental powers back into submission) could emerge. His strategy against these allies was to defeat them rapidly in detail – that is, before they could combine their forces completely. He therefore aimed first at Austria and the Russian army moving to join the Austrians, planning to strike directly at the Austrian capital, Vienna, to knock Austria out of the coalition. His operational execution of this plan was brilliant: he marched the Grande Armée from the coast into Austria so quickly that he surrounded one Austrian army completely, virtually without a fight, and moved toward the waiting combined Austro-Russian force beyond Vienna. When he got to grips with that army, he executed a grand tactical maneuver that involved exposing his own right flank to attack, drawing allied reserves, followed by a decisive assault through the weakened allied center that split the allied army and shattered it. The tactics used by the French army included concentrated artillery bombardment in support of infantry attacks in both line and column as well as cavalry charges. Napoleon's success in this campaign and in the following one against Prussia in 1806 was so thorough that it allowed him to begin to conceive of a new grand strategy for defeating Britain that involved a continent-wide embargo against British trade, the source of British wealth and power. This example shows how the various levels of military analysis are usefully distinct but also in practice shade into each other and relate to each other.

Concepts relating to the "art of war"

Though the boundaries between them are sometimes unclear, there is general agreement about these levels of analysis. The same cannot necessarily be said for the major principles and concepts relating to the art of war. There is no definitive handbook of strategic, operational, or tactical principles because so much of successful management of armed forces in the field depends on adaptation and improvisation in the face of unexpected developments. This is not to say that there are no generally agreed principles or guidelines. Generals since Sunzi have usually agreed that the strategic and operational offensive is advantageous, for example, because it allows the attacker to exercise more influence over the time and place of battle and to concentrate his forces, whereas the defender must spread his forces to guard against multiple possible targets of attack. Conversely, in many times and places the tactical defensive has been the advantaged position on the battlefield, though there are more exceptions to this "rule," proving that no rule of military operations is ironclad and that no concise list of The Most Important Rules is possible.

On the other hand, simply listing and explaining all the terms commonly used in analyzing military actions is an impossible task in a short historiographical survey – there are too many of them. And a complete survey is probably unnecessary even for a beginning student since many terms are relatively self-explanatory: the notion of a *reserve* or the distinction between a war of *attrition* and one of *annihilation* hardly need technical definitions, for example. Those terms that do have specialist or technical meanings are usually explained in the literature in which they occur: a *curtain of maneuver* may not be an intuitively obvious concept, for example, but Clifford Rogers explains it in describing Henry of Lancaster's Bergerac campaign of 1345.[7]

If a complete glossary is neither possible nor necessary, we can still offer some rough characterizations about art of war terminology. First, there tend to be terms specific to each level of analysis outlined in the previous section. An *enfilade*, or subjecting an enemy line to flanking fields of fire, is an exclusively tactical term, for instance. There are also more general principles applicable at almost any level. *Interior lines*, which describes the situation where a force on the interior of a (semi)circle can reach any point on the circle more quickly than a force operating outside the circle – on exterior lines – though usually an operational or strategic concept, can be applied at the grand tactical level. Second, we can make a distinction between terms that are largely descriptive and those that carry more normative connotations – that is, those that tend to be more prescriptive principles. *Line ahead* and *line abreast* are terms that simply describe the two major sorts of organized formations ships assumed for battles (before the advent of naval airpower, anyway), for example, though in many eighteenth-century navies line ahead was the prescribed rule that captains had to follow. *Economy of force*, however, while it can describe the disposition of troops in a particular campaign, is more often presented as a normative principle of operations that says, in one form, that the minimum possible forces *should* be allocated to peripheral theaters of a campaign so that the greatest possible concentration of force can be achieved at the point of decision. In another form favored by the US army, it means taking objectives without unnecessary squandering of resources, including lives. Of course, especially in military history aimed at future commanders, descriptive and normative uses of terms interact constantly as the historian draws normative lessons from descriptions of historical events. Finally, the most technical terms usually relate to technologies and practices peculiar to specific services of the armed forces (army, navy, airforce, marines) and to branches or specialists within services (armor, artillery, cavalry, and so forth) and are thus the terms farthest from "universal principles" and most likely to change over time.

Concepts relating to the practice of war

One of the major trends in the writing of military history, as we have already seen, has been the move away from art of war studies and operational histories toward more socially and economically embedded examinations of the use of armed force. As a result, the study of *logistics* has come into much more prominence than before. Looking at logistics, or how armed forces are supplied both in peacetime and on campaign, has highlighted both the limitations of some traditional art of war approaches by showing how significantly the strategic choices supposedly open to commanders were constrained by the potential availability of food and water sources, as well as the practical meaning of some traditional concepts (what does a *line of communication* mean to an army that lives off the land, whether by buying, requisitioning, or plundering supplies?).[8] That same focus on how armies fed themselves opened up some of the vast field of research into the impact of war on society, and in research on more modern warfare has entailed new looks at the *economics of warfare* and the relationship of a state's industrial capacity to its ability to make war. Many of these conceptual strands come together in examinations of modern *military industrial complexes*. President Dwight D. Eisenhower gave that name to the process, observable long before he coined the term, in which the special interests of arms manufacturers and suppliers become (or threaten to become) economically influential enough, at least in shaping government policy, that the state manufactures permanent states of "war" (real, threatened, or, if necessary, invented) in order to justify continued appropriations to suppliers.[9]

Important concepts also attach to the study of military systems in terms of their organization and administration. The *table of organization* of most modern armies, though it has some conceptual roots in Roman army organization and analogues in other ancient military systems, in particular classical Chinese armies, traces its direct lineage back to the seventeenth century's *regimental system*, in which permanent regiments of infantry not only became the organizational backbone of European armies but attained such institutional permanence that they began to create their own institutional cultures and to generate their own regimental histories. By now the hierarchy of units and the officers that command them in modern armies is similar enough around the world (see table 3.1 with the example of the US army) as to seem almost "natural," but application of modern unit terminology by analogy to the organizations of past armies carries significant dangers

Table 3.1 US army unit hierarchy

Standard Symbol	Combat Formations			Administrative Formations
XXXXXX	Theater			Command
XXXXX	Army Group			
XXXX	Army			Branch
XXX	Corps			
XX	Division			Regiment
X	Brigade			
III	Group		Regiment	
II	Battalion		Squadron	
I	Company	Battery	Troop	
●●●	Platoon/ Detachment			
●●	Section			
●	Squad			
Ø	Team/ Crew			
■	Installation			

Source: Federation of Army Scientists. Online at: <http://www.fas.org/man/dod–101/army/unit/index.html>

of imposing a shape on historical evidence that it doesn't really have: some armies, such as Qing China's, had unit hierarchies that arose out of very different sorts of organizational structures and imperatives; while others, such as most pre-modern armies including any medieval European army, had no table of organization, no permanent units, and no formal system, regimental or otherwise, at all.

Indeed, even when they have similar formal organizations, the world's armies past and present exhibit a wide range of institutional cultures and styles of *command and control*, a crucial aspect of translating formal organization into effective fighting force, as recent studies of armed forces from the perspective of organizational theory have shown. Military institutional cultures vary not just within branches of the armed services and by how closely they reflect the broader cultures from which they are drawn,[10] but in how they implement decision-making at various levels of the organization. Finally, any system of command and control is both dependent on what sort of *intelligence*, or information about enemy forces, movements, and intentions, is available to decision-makers within it – the unreliability of which for most of history is reflected in the common Clausewitzian phrase "the fog of war" – and to his related concept of *friction*: that basic tasks always take longer and never go as smoothly as planners would like to assume, a notion reflected in the military origins of the word "snafu," from "situation normal, all fouled up" (to use the polite F-word version).

It would be useful to be able to add a standard set of terms denoting the types of armies that have existed historically, categorized by how they are raised and what their relationship to their states and societies are. Unfortunately, there are plenty of common terms – mercenary, conscript, professional, volunteer, militia, and so on – but no widely agreed-on classification. Historians will undoubtedly continue to argue and attempt to classify types of armies for some time to come.

War and Society: Interdisciplinary Influences

The traditional and more recent concepts relating to military art and practice outlined in the previous section intersect with a range of techniques for understanding the past. The influence of social and cultural history and the expansion of the field of military history through war and society studies have added significantly to the military historian's methodological toolkit. Military historians increasingly recognize that to understand a relationship as complex and reciprocal as that between a society and its armed forces requires as wide a range of data and models as possible. This section will outline some of the academic fields outside history that have contributed notable insights and intellectual techniques to areas of military history, as well as those for which military history questions have become important within that discipline.

Anthropology

Anthropologists have studied warfare among the rapidly disappearing simple societies (tribes and hunter-gatherer bands) of the modern world. This has resulted in the development of theories about a number of aspects of warfare more generally, though none of them has been accepted completely and most are subject to serious debate. Some have to do with defining warfare itself as distinct from other sorts of less organized violence such as murder or vendetta. The anthropologist Hugh Turney-High, for example, proposed the concept of the "military horizon," the level of warfare and social complexity above which intrapersonal violence becomes true warfare.[11] The debate about what constitutes true warfare has become entangled with an even more vexed question hotly debated by paleoanthropologists (anthropologists who study early humans through the archaeological record; we will discuss archaeology in a moment): what are the origins of war? Two major positions have emerged in this debate. On the one hand, some see warfare as an inevitable expression of aggressive human nature and claim to see evidence for organized forms of violence far back in the archaeological record (as well as assuming its existence when the evidence is nonexistent). The other position takes a more benign view of human nature, stressing the cooperative aspect of humans as social animals, and reads the archaeological record to show that evidence for warfare only appears about 10,000 years ago and coincides with settled (usually agricultural) societies and the hierarchical political organizations that they spawned.[12] As with many debates about the past, this one has a modern political dimension, which may be simplistically summed up as pitting those who say "war is inevitable, we must prepare for it" against those who say "war is a social-cultural construct and can be eliminated." Less controversially, anthropologists have contributed data and theories about the intimate connection between warfare (at many levels of complexity) and the construction of gender identities and roles, for notions of manhood and rituals of passage to adulthood among males have often been associated with fighting.

Archaeology

The evidence for paleoanthropologists' debate about the origins of war comes from archaeology in the form of human skeletal remains that show signs of human violence (arrow heads embedded in rib cages and so forth) and excavations of the earliest fortifications, walls around settlements being a good indicator of both violent threat and the social organization required to meet it. The history of warfare in all periods benefits from the material evidence uncovered by archaeology. Most obviously, the weapons and armor that are discovered in grave sites (often as part of ritual burial furniture) and at battlefields, and the illustrations of warriors and warfare carved into buildings and monuments, give historians a view into the appearance of past warfare. The brutal effectiveness of the weapons of hand-to-hand combat show up in the cloven skulls and severed limbs of battlefield finds such as that at Wisby in Sweden, the site of a medieval battle.[13] Archaeology at the Little Big Horn battlefield (1876) verified that US General Custer's troops were outgunned by Sioux with repeating rifles, as well as outnumbered; it also indicates that Custer and the 210 men with him held out longer than was claimed in the self-serving testimony of subordinates conscious of criticism for not going to Custer's aid.[14] Naval (underwater) archaeology has provided invaluable evidence for ship types and construction techniques, especially for ancient Mediterranean and Viking ships. These insights have been furthered by the work of experimental archaeologists who reconstruct ancient weaponry using historical techniques. This has given historians a far better appreciation of the amount of labor that went into making chain-mail armor, for example, or what sort of destruction a counterweight trebuchet could do to a castle's stone wall. Perhaps the most spectacular piece of experimental archaeology has been the reconstruction of a classical Athenian trireme, a warship driven by three banks of oars, by a group of Greek, British, and American archaeologists. The *Olympias* clarified many disputes about how such ships must have been built that had been unclear based on the surviving ancient evidence.[15] But perhaps the most significant insights that archaeology has given military historians has been into demography and levels of soil fertility and subsistence, both of which topics are vital to understanding the logistical constraints that have shaped patterns of warfare since its (disputed) beginning.

Political science

Political scientists have often been concerned with many of the same questions as historians, though their focus tends to be on the more recent past and present. But the wealth of contemporary data political scientists often have at their disposal, as well as the construction of the field as a social science, has meant that political scientists have more readily approached their questions through the construction of models that attempt to isolate and quantify the crucial variables of a problem. Historians, some of whom see themselves as social scientists but many of whom prefer to see history as one of the humanities, have mostly been suspicious of political science models (with the notable exception of Marxist historians, which has simply exacerbated the suspicion of the rest). The historian's inclination to see the particulars and exceptions embedded in specific narratives clashes with the generalizations and simplifications necessary for constructing broad schemas and models. Nevertheless, both fields have benefited from cross-fertilization as historians provide evidence for political science models and those models in turn influence historians' interpretations. Political scientists have made especially notable contributions to theories of the causes of wars and to the currently important examination of the connection between war and state formation.[16]

Sociology, psychology, economics

The insights of the other major social science fields have also found their way into military history in various ways. In a tradition going back to Max Weber, sociologists have modeled and classified types of organizations and bureaucracies; the findings have been applied to military systems and the organizational differences between different armies.[17] Modern psychology has provided valuable tools and concepts for analyzing individual and group performance. This has included studies of pathologies whose appearance in modern warfare has prompted historians to look for their analogues in the past, including shell shock and behaviors reminiscent of "berserking," the battle madness of Viking warriors (which may have a deep Indo-European ancestry).[18] It has also been consciously applied, in both historical studies and in modern training methods, to styles of leadership and motivation and their effect on unit cohesion and effectiveness and has informed the whole "face of battle" line of military history, as we have already noted. Finally, economics has a long history of association with history, as economic history is a venerable field in its own right. Economic theory and methods have been used to analyze the costs and benefits of warfare, and in combination with numismatics has provided insight into the state financial systems and broader economies that supported military systems.

The application of social science models, however, which are often dependent on fairly substantial runs of data if they are to provide useful conclusions, raises a problem of evidence. Very few historical eras and regions provide the sort of reliable quantitative data upon which analytical techniques usefully grouped under the rubric of *cliometrics* (from Clio, the Muse of History) can operate. The misleading precision of numbers can hide their lack of accuracy, and in the absence of any reliable statistical evidence much cliometric analysis can devolve into little more than educated guesswork in which foundational assumptions assume a crucial role. But where evidence is abundant and reliable, statistical analysis and mathematical modeling using the abundance of modern computing power can shed light even on unexpectedly distant subjects in military history.[19]

Cultural theory

Not that historians' usual narrative (or at least descriptive) sources are unproblematic. Military historians, like all historians (though perhaps more slowly and reluctantly as a group), have had to take account of the insights into reading and interpreting such sources offered by the theorists of the loose collective of postmodernism, deconstructionism, postcoloniality, and cultural theory.[20] We have already mentioned above the impact that performative theory is having on notions of the construction of cultural identities and their impact on ideas about causation. It is also such theory that has brought questions of gender (especially the construction of masculinity) to the fore both via anthropology and directly. Both deconstructionism and postcolonial theory emphasize reading sources for multiple voices in a culture, deconstructionism by reading between the lines, with attention to the power relationships enacted by any piece of writing, in order to recover opposing points of view, postcolonial theory by stressing the role and voice of the "subaltern," those on the receiving end of structures of colonial rule. The general impact of such emphases on other voices (and voices of the Other) cannot but be useful to a field such as military history that is particularly prone to the triumphalism inherent in the old saying that "the winners write history," since the winners were often victorious militarily.

The overall effect on military history of these various interdisciplinary concepts, methods and theories has been to bring greater depth and sophistication to studies of military systems and actions, especially in terms of their relationship to and mutual impact on the societies that employ military force, while at the same time beginning to draw military historical material more into the mainstream of historical studies. The process is still, however, in its early stages and there remain many fruitful paths of research to be explored from this angle.

Global History and Comparative Methodology

The same can be said about the last significant conceptual change affecting military history currently, the rise of global perspectives and comparative methods. Though just as recent, if not more so, than the influence of interdisciplinary theories connected to war and society studies, "globalizing" the study of warfare has been somewhat less controversial and less subject to resistance than applying concepts from gender studies and otherwise transforming it via cultural and social history. This is probably because of the two related sides of the context for this change.

First, the idea that we are living in an age of globalization has vast political and cultural currency. This has been matched by tremendous growth, in academic history and in secondary and college-level teaching, of world history as a subfield (with world historians happy to point out how current takes on globalization often short-sightedly ignore previous episodes of globalization in world history). While much world history has treated military history as cursorily as have more traditional fields, inevitably some historians have begun to work the fertile fields at the intersection of the new military history and the new world history. Second, some of the impetus for this work has come from the contemporary need by professional military personnel for globally based analysis. It is increasingly clear these days that warfare (including the arms trade and the economic infrastructures, legal and illegal, that fund weapons acquisition and the waging of war or, as in the case of oil reserves, provide pretexts for waging war) is itself increasingly global in exactly the ways that world historians have begun to examine for other phenomena. That is, while there is a globally interconnected system within which warfare can take place, the conflict this system generates involves very little of the meeting of politically and technologically similar and reasonably well-matched major states – the sort of global warfare that characterized the two world wars and the Cold War confrontation between the superpowers. (This is not to say that those wars were not world historical or global phenomena, but that they could be fit within the conceptual frameworks already developed for the analysis of interstate warfare and politics in European history since the mid-seventeenth century. Indeed, World War I was basically a European civil war whose scope and implications were global simply because of the scale of European colonial holdings; the same is partly true, though with a significantly greater independently Asian component, of World War II and much of the Cold War, counting the US as a North Atlantic power, if not strictly speaking a European one.) Rather, a global system that truly connects many disparate places generates asymmetrical, unconventional, low-level, or internecine conflicts that do not conform to standard expectations for great power warfare militarily, politically, or culturally and so must be viewed in new ways, ways that world historians specialize in. That these sorts of armed conflicts necessarily involve complex social and cultural factors contributes, incidentally, to the utility and spread of the social and cultural theories discussed in the previous section. Jeremy Black, in his important book *Rethinking Military History*, makes a strong case that global perspectives and their associated methods and concerns should be, and increasingly are, central to the modern practice of military history. He argues that in addition to Eurocentrism, military history needs to address a range of problematic constructs including technological determinism, an emphasis on (western) paradigm/diffusion models, a near exclusive focus on state-to-state conflicts, and an artificial separation of land and sea warfare.[21]

The reader should not be surprised at this point, however, when we say that comparative history, though necessary and welcomed, is by no means unproblematic in application. It depends on careful functional analysis of "objects" – whether those be military units, technology or systems, political structures, or mechanisms of social control, cultural production, and so on – that are carefully chosen and defined so as to be productively comparable. Standard terminology, especially in translation, is, unhelpfully, likely to be misleading in this case: the functional roles of a Byzantine and a medieval Japanese "emperor" were very different, for example, and so comparisons of "emperorship" potentially misleading.[22] The imposition of standard modern terminology for military units on historical armies, mentioned above, is another example of the dangers that can beset careless comparative analysis.

These terminological difficulties are in some sense a special case of a more pervasive and distorting tendency in comparative history of "centrism." Centrism as we define it here occurs when one case (society, pattern, whatever) out of many is used as the norm or standard for comparison, especially if the choice is unconscious, politically motivated, or simply lazy. The most common centrism, in both practice and allegation, in current historical literature is Eurocentrism, in which European norms, terms, concepts, developmental patterns, and so forth are held up as the standard by which phenomena from other regions are to be judged, usually unfavorably – an intellectual tendency with deep roots in the colonial dominance of European states in the nineteenth and earlier twentieth centuries. (Black's *Rethinking Military History* is particularly aimed at the Eurocentrism of much military history.) Aside from the problematic political and cultural implications involved in denigrating the historical experience of non-European peoples, the problem with centrisms for comparative history is that they inevitably lead to distortion of the historical record as evidence from non-centric cases is shoehorned into the conceptual categories established by the centric case. An example from military history is the concept of "feudalism," a supposed type of political-military organization as well as a supposed developmental stage, either specifically military or more generally, in Marxist terms, in socioeconomic history. Its military meaning is so problematic even within Europe that European medievalists have largely abandoned it, but it continues as a category of analysis (or at least a name) in comparative analysis that probably does more to confuse than it does to enlighten.[23]

Aside from these conceptual difficulties, comparative history suffers from the practical difficulty of constructing appropriate comparisons (an issue closely related to our philosophical discussion of universals above) and the even more practical problem of comparable data. Sources from different places and times, created each for its own purpose in a particular cultural milieu and informed by particular cultural traditions, necessarily pay attention to different things and so give different pictures of their piece of the past, even when the nominal topic (warfare, say) is the same. Constructing useful comparisons from such disparate data is a challenging proposition.

Yet the challenge is well worth attempting because, like the interdisciplinary theories and concepts of social and cultural history, comparative history yields undeniable benefits.[24] Comparative analysis can bring new patterns in historical evidence to light, stimulate the posing of new questions, and sometimes contribute new data to questions that cannot be decided decisively from within just one tradition. In some ways, comparative history provides the opportunity to run the closest equivalent historians can have to a "controlled experiment." The impact of the introduction of gunpowder on European warfare, for instance, looks very different when set in the context of the global spread of gunpowder weaponry; the late introduction of guns to Japan, a society comparable in important ways to Europe in the sixteenth century, provides an especially useful comparative case for study.[25] Another way to look at the problem is that the value of a "global perspective" is promoted by world historians as well as by contemporary business analysts and strategic planners. But while a significant part of having a global perspective is viewing the earth's history as a whole and seeing the various systems (most obviously economic) that tie the world together as global phenomena, a global perspective also necessarily involves the ability to compare and so better understand the different components that make up a global system. This is as true of military history, past and present, as of any other field of historical inquiry.

Conclusions

Military history, like all fields of history, is philosophically diverse and methodologically rich. Although it has been (and is still often viewed as) one of the most traditional subfields of history, resistant to new perspectives and as a result less "respectable" than mainstream academic subfields, much of the best work in recent military history shares fully with the larger profession in the conceptual and methodological advances offered by social scientific disciplines, cultural and literary studies, and world historical perspectives. The utility of these conceptual additions to the military historian's intellectual arsenal insures that their influence will continue to grow and that students will need to understand and appreciate their place in the practice of military history.

4
Current Controversies

Given the many possible perspectives historians bring to their work, as well as the different methodological and philosophical approaches they can apply to their view of the past, it may seem surprising that historians ever agree on their interpretations of the evidence. But in fact, history is much more a cooperative venture in which separate interpretations complement each other, creating a more rounded and complete picture of the past, than it is a competitive one. Even significant change in historical interpretations often comes about gradually and as a matter of evolving consensus, as the perspectives and interests of an entire generation of historians give way to those of a new generation.

Still, controversies do arise, often around the most significant and groundbreaking issues. The nature of academia, indeed, encourages new interpretations and thus arguments. This chapter will explore some of the most prominent current controversies in the field of military history, analyzing what the issues are and why they are important. We will, almost inevitably, present these issues in a way that some will disagree with, as our own opinions about the issues presented will color our interpretation of the argument. But the attempt is to present a dispassionate analysis of the controversies, not to argue one side or the other.

Historical controversies usually come in two types, often overlapping. First, there are those arguments arising about the "facts" of the past, recognizing always that facts are only significant in the context of an interpretive framework. Such arguments usually arise from a shortage of reliable evidence and may be settled by the discovery of new evidence, though a total lack of evidence rarely engenders controversy since there is nothing to argue from. (History, again, is a field whose interpretations are grounded in and thus constrained by evidence, which largely accounts for the degree of agreement historians reach despite the incentive to argue.) "Factual" arguments may include questions about physical realities of the past: the efficacy (killing power) of the longbow on fourteenth- and fifteenth-century battlefields, for example, has been debated.[1] Did it win battles by killing men and horses, or did its effectiveness derive from its ability to channel and disrupt enemy movements and shatter morale? But they may also include arguments about the nature of an historical "fact." Terence Zuber has recently and vehemently called into question the reality of the Schlieffen Plan, the supposed blueprint for Germany's invasion of France in World War I, for instance, characterizing it as an invention of historians. Others have just as vehemently argued for its reality.[2] In most cases, however, arguments about specific facts are by their nature fairly limited in scope and impact.

It is arguments over interpretations of huge, complex events and developments that can engage the interests of large camps of historians. It is these sorts of controversies that this chapter will analyze. Such controversies show several things. First, that military history is a vital, evolving field. Second, they are reminders of the creative tension in all historical study between understanding the past on its own terms and understanding the past in light of present concerns – that is, that current politics, broadly defined, unavoidably shapes how history is studied. And finally, that constant reinterpretation is central to history and is the responsibility of every student of history. In other words, one should read these arguments not for which side is "right," since even if there is a "winning" side the winners will find themselves reinterpreted in the future, but rather for how and why historians argue.

Military Revolutions

The biggest area of contention in military history today concerns the idea of "military revolutions." A "military revolution," broadly speaking, is a period of rapid change in how warfare is conducted with results so significant that they change the course of historical development far beyond the military sphere. The fundamental argument is about whether they exist.

The original "military revolution" was named by Michael Roberts in a series of lectures delivered in 1955.[3] His thesis was that the introduction of effective musketry around 1560 led to a century of far-reaching transformation in which the key figure was the Swedish king Gustavus Adolphus (Roberts was an historian of Sweden). Guns necessitated more linear battlefield tactics to make most effective use of the new firepower. Linear tactics required better trained and drilled troops, which led to the creation of standing armies and allowed new, more aggressive strategies. This pushed up the size of armies. At this point, the need for larger, better trained armies led governments to reorganize their administrations in order to raise and support such forces more effectively. It was this development – what Roberts argued for as the foundation of early modern state formation and thus the origin of modern national states – that gave Roberts's thesis its wider significance.

Though noted by some military historians, and despite its Big History claims, Roberts's ideas failed to make much impact for 20 years, an indication of the distance separating military history from mainstream historical debate during that time. Geoffrey Parker revived the idea in a 1976 article that actually critiqued Roberts's ideas, arguing instead for an earlier revolutionary turning point and a slightly different initial cause.[4] This inspired a small explosion of articles in the mid-1980s questioning almost every aspect of Roberts's original thesis in detail – especially the supposed tactical changes that lay at the heart of Roberts's chain of causation – and at times questioning the very concept of revolutionary change. But Parker returned to the subject decisively with his 1988 book *The Military Revolution*, noted above in chapter 2, revising and expanding the ideas sketched in his 1976 article. Parker, an historian of Spain, saw little reason to rate Gustavus' tactics as more effective than those of the famed Spanish *tercios* that had already worked out an effective coordination of firepower and pikes by the early sixteenth century. He therefore moved the key revolutionary moment up almost a century, to the 1490s. He argued that the crucial gunpowder weaponry for stimulating change was not muskets but cannon, in particular in their devastating effect on medieval fortifications demonstrated in the French invasion of Italy in 1494. The invention by Italian engineers in the 1520s of the *trace italienne*, the geometric style of fortification designed to resist cannonade, restored the balance of offense and defense, but the range of cannonry meant that the geometry of sieges expanded vastly. It was this, Parker claimed, that necessitated tremendous increases in army size and the consequent effects in stimulating state building that Roberts had already noted. Furthermore, he connected the combination of gunpowder, *trace italienne* fortifications, and drilled armies raised by strong states to a dramatic rise in European power globally between 1500 and 1800. In short, cannon stimulated a military revolution that gave birth not just to the modern state but to European hegemony in the world.

It was the significance of these claims, presented clearly and elegantly, and backed by substantial scholarship, that allowed Parker's book to insert military history squarely into mainstream historical discussions. His thesis modified and gave more concrete form to similar claims about the impact of military technology and capitalism on world historical patterns that William McNeill, the dean of world historians, had explored a few years earlier in his book *The Pursuit of Power*.[5] Military history thus became associated with the rise of world history that was occurring at that time. His formulation of the military revolution idea did not, however, go unchallenged. Among a rising tide of focused studies that built on and questioned specific aspects of Parker's thesis, the work of Jeremy Black stands out as the third major formulation of the early modern military revolution idea. Black, an eighteenth-century specialist and one of the most productive and important military historians working in the world today, took Roberts's military revolution thesis in the opposite direction from Parker chronologically and causally.[6] He argued first that both Roberts and, even more, Parker had placed the significant military changes in European warfare too early. It was only *after* 1660, he said, and really after 1720, that advances in European military techniques coalesced into a style of warfare that was noticeably superior to those of Europe's neighbors (especially the Ottoman Turks). And the word "techniques" is significant here, for he argued that it was not superior technology but superior battlefield discipline and maneuverability – abilities made possible by drill – that distinguished European armies after 1720. This reflected his inversion of the causal elements earlier in the process. Where Roberts and Parker had argued from new technology to changes in state power, Black argued that it was only after the reconsolidation of political and social power among European kings and their aristocracies, possible only with the ending of the Wars of Religion and the internal factionalism they so often fostered, that governments could harness the potential of new technologies. In short, he put social change as a necessary prior condition for the effective use of technology. Black's thesis was important, therefore, both for complexifying the notion of causation embedded in arguments about the military revolution and for bringing careful comparative analysis from a global perspective to the debate.

By the early 1990s, the idea of an early modern military revolution had gained such force and currency (even if its major proponents did not agree on what, precisely, caused and constituted the revolution) that the concept began to metastasize throughout the body of military historiography, extending well beyond early modern Europe even as debates about details of military transformation in early modern Europe continued to rage.[7] The most closely related extension of the idea was the claim, advanced first by Clifford Rogers in 1993,[8] that the transformations of the early modern period depended on a prior set of transformations that had affected late medieval warfare after about 1300. That set of changes had brought infantry to the fore after a long period of cavalry dominance on the battlefields of Europe and had, slightly later and especially in the form of the English longbow (Rogers is an Edward III scholar), emphasized infantry firepower. Rogers dubbed these changes the "Infantry Revolution." He also identified a prior stage in the development of artillery that he claimed laid the groundwork for Parker's starting point, and proposed a model drawn from evolutionary biology of "punctuated equilibrium evolution" as opposed to revolution to characterize a set of changes in European warfare that now seemed to stretch from 1300 to the mid-1700s. Ten years later, Kenneth Chase set the idea of an "infantry revolution" in a global analysis that stressed the geographic importance of facing (or not having to face) steppe nomadic cavalry in the rise of infantry-based military systems that could make effective use of gunpowder weapons.[9]

But the even more powerful extension of the early modern military revolution debate came with the application of the abstract concept of a "military revolution" – especially in its Roberts–Parker form as a technologically initiated transformation of military practice with broad implications for the course of history generally – to other eras of history. "Military revolutions" were newly identified in ancient history, associated with the spread of bronze metallurgy and, especially, with the rise of chariot-riding elites, and later with the rise of iron metallurgy and mass infantry armies (the first "infantry revolution").[10] Significant and well-acknowledged military transformations of recent history were re-christened as revolutions: World War I saw a firepower revolution, World War II a maneuver revolution. Suddenly, military revolutions were everywhere.

The extension of this sort that generated (and continues to generate) the most debate posited a military revolution that its proponents claim is currently ongoing. Called the "Revolution in Military Affairs" (RMA) by those theorizing it, it actually had its roots in Soviet military theory in the 1970s and 1980s. Soviet military analysts who observed the use of early precision-guided munitions by the US at the end of the conflict in Vietnam began to write about a "military technical revolution" that could change the military balance between the two superpowers. American analysts picked up on this, and the literature converged with the "military revolution" historical literature to produce the Revolution in Military Affairs. RMA theorists claim revolutionary implications for linked technologies of communications and airpower.[11] The application of these technologies, it is said, are revolutionizing battlefield action, simultaneously lifting the "fog of war" and making for a virtually bloodless battlefield (at least for the side capable of deploying an unmatchable superiority in such technology – major RMA theorists have tended to be from the former USSR and now from the US[12]). RMA writing is less clear about the broader implications of these military developments, in large part because they have not yet happened, which is one reason its theorists chose to distinguish their "Revolution in Military Affairs" from "military revolutions" that have analyzable historical consequences: the concept is intentionally more narrow. One way of looking at the relationship of RMAs to military revolutions in a broader historical context is that a military revolution occurs after a series of "anticipatory RMAs" have occurred. The amount of debate this extension of the military revolution idea has generated is therefore proportional not to its significance as an historical topic but to its currency: the positions staked out in the RMA debate have direct policy implications for military spending and force composition.

The many directions in which the debates about military revolutions have expanded mean that this new paradigm has subsumed some older ongoing debates in military history. The RMA debate in this light is partly an extension in new conceptual clothing of a long-running twentieth-century debate about the efficacy of airpower, a debate that goes back to the strategic bombing theories of Giulio Douhet and Billy Mitchell in the 1920s. Airpower proponents have long envisioned wars won at very low cost in (friendly) casualties through strategic bombing, and have long met resistance from theorists (and reality) who argue the ongoing need for conventional ground and naval forces as well.[13] The RMA literature is also interesting in largely ignoring the other side of this older historiography of strategic bombing, the side that debated (and continues to debate) not just the actual efficacy but the morality of this sort of warfare.[14] This debate extends to arguments about the dropping of atomic bombs on Hiroshima and Nagasaki (two very different cases, in fact, in terms of this debate) and to the potential effects and morality of mutually assured nuclear annihilation. The advent of the nuclear age itself is a case for inclusion as a military revolution. Older historiographical controversies have also been subsumed under arguments about military revolutions. Arguments about an "infantry revolution" of the fourteenth century form a counterpoint to older, technologically based arguments about the origins of cavalry dominance in medieval European warfare that saw the introduction of the stirrup as the basis not just for the tactical ascendancy of mounted warriors but also of the social system ("feudalism," so called, itself an historiographical point of contention that we will explore briefly below) that supposedly arose to support such warriors.[15]

What general philosophical and methodological issues underpin and inform the various related debates that make up "military revolution" historiography? Several stand out. At a level that almost reduces to pure semantics, there is the question that arises repeatedly in this literature of what constitutes a "revolution"? Some have questioned whether an "event" that stretches in several stages over several hundred years can properly be characterized as a revolution; this is the concern that led Rogers to propose "punctuated equilibrium evolution" as an alternate way of characterizing the military transformations of European warfare between 1300 and 1750. Such concerns are mirrored by similar concerns about terms such as Industrial Revolution and Agricultural Revolution, for example, though such cases also point out that many historians are happy to apply the term "revolution" to "events" extending over not just hundreds but thousands of years.

The aspect of this issue that is not pedantically semantic is the question of whether the various military revolutions that have been identified, including the paradigmatic early modern European one, actually exist as historical phenomena or are simply misleading historiographical constructs. The fundamental theoretical problem here concerns the dichotomy, possibly false, between continuity and disruptive change – between evolution and revolution – in conceptualizing the shape of the past. This is a potentially false dichotomy because in many ways the difference between gradualism and dramatic change is simply a matter of the chronological scale at which one examines events, as Daniel Dennett has pointed out about Stephen Jay Gould's original biological formulation of punctuated equilibrium.[16] That is, what looks at a very large scale like sudden change – the rapid shift, compared to several million years of hunting and gathering, to agriculture in some areas between 12,000 and 8,000 years ago, for example – looks at a smaller scale like a slow and gradual process. (The true dichotomy is between gradualism – at various scales – and what Gould calls "saltation": sudden discontinuous leaps (Latin *saltus*, a jump or leap). This is the dichotomy that separates biologists and historians on one side from religious fundamentalists' views of both biological and historical evolution on the other.) But there is a strong case against military revolutions that questions whether the sudden and transformative changes claimed for them exist even at smaller chronological scales. That is (and this is the position Black takes, for instance, on the question of whether there was an early modern military revolution), there is gradualism all the way down, and trying to isolate a revolutionary moment "when things changed" is usually impossible. (The dawn of the atomic age may be an exception.)

Gradualist views of change are usually associated in the literature with questions about causation. One of the appealing things about military revolution arguments is the relative clarity and simplicity of the chain of causation they propose: a new technology appears and the consequences follow with unvarying logic. In its most simplistic form, this is classic technological determinism, though few of the best military revolution theories are quite that simplistic. Still, technological change tends to lie at the heart of almost every military revolution thesis, ancient, medieval, early modern, or modern. The problem, as many critics have pointed out, is that the consequences of new technology do not follow with unvarying logic. Rather, the impact of a new technology depends heavily on the social and cultural environment into which it is introduced. Thus, the introduction of gunpowder technology had very different implications for warfare in sixteenth-century Angola and sixteenth-century Japan, and the similarity of the effects of gunpowder in the latter case to those in Europe should be explained not by the inherent tendencies of the technology but by the similar paths that political and social developments had taken in both Europe and Japan prior to the introduction of guns.[17] The trouble for proponents of such views is that complex, contingent, multicausal arguments that start from nuanced views of social structure, economic activity, and cultural tendencies are harder to explain clearly than monocausal formulas, whether technology or, in Kenneth Chase's view of infantry revolutions and the spread of gunpowder, geography is the single cause. (This may explain why Parker's formulation of the military revolution idea achieved far greater impact than did McNeill's slightly earlier but less clearly formulated take on the same broad subject.)

An interesting comment on this historiographical tendency may be seen in the fate of the nineteenth century in the military revolution literature. A relatively short period (1830–1914) of undeniably intense and significant technological change in military weaponry, the nineteenth century has nevertheless mostly escaped being labeled as any sort of military revolution. Why? Perhaps because there is no single technological breakthrough that characterizes the period, but rather a gradually accelerating process of technological experimentation. This in turn emphasizes the common understanding of the period as one of deep economic, social, and cultural transformation (that is, of the coming of the Industrial Revolution), and the recognition that military change was simply one aspect of that deeper set of changes. Military technology in this view was simply one branch of industrial technology. And industrial technology from Marxist and increasingly many other historiographical perspectives is not the cause but one consequence, one product with further consequences, of the socioeconomic transformations that produced the Industrial Revolution. In other words, the nineteenth century confounds simplistic, technologically driven views of military transformation, and so fits uneasily into the military revolution paradigm. As a result, it tends to be relegated in that literature to a position of denouement (the European dominance of the nineteenth century was simply the playing out of European superiority established between 1500 and 1800 as a consequence of the military revolution, in Parker's formulation) or of foundation (industrialization having been well established by the early twentieth century, it can disappear into the background, leaving the stage free for revolutions based on tanks, planes, and electronic communications equipment). Put another way, nineteenth-century military technology is seen in that literature to have led to tactical stalemate in the trenches of World War I that necessitated new technological revolutions to break the deadlock.

It may also be relevant that the various technological trans-formations of the nineteenth century eventuated not just in European conquests globally (far more pervasively, in fact, than between 1500 and 1800), but in the undeniable disaster of 1914–18. For there is, apart from examinations of so-called military revolutions in ancient history (and even in some of those), a more or less explicit connection between accounts of advances in military technology and accounts of the "rise of the West," to use McNeill's famous phrase. This leads us to another deep controversy in contemporary military history, the question of "western" exceptionalism, that is relevant to the questions of military revolutions, whether they exist, and what the real impact of military transformation has been. We shall turn to that controversy in the next section.

Whatever one's position on the question of military revolu-tions in history (and it is probably clear at this point that we are among the skeptics concerning their existence in this realm), the importance of military revolutions as an historio-graphical phenomenon cannot be denied. The idea has been responsible for military history's re-entry into the mainstream historical big picture, to the extent that sections on the mili-tary transformation of early modern Europe, whether called a revolution or not, are now common in survey textbooks. And because the concept has been applied across such a broad chronological sweep of history, it has in some ways provided a conceptual common ground where the somewhat diffuse interests of pre-modern or pre-industrial military historians and their modernist colleagues can meet and productively debate, exchange, and cross-fertilize. In short, it has been, for military history as a field, a most healthy controversy.

"The West": Exceptionalism and Dominance?

If the military revolution debate has been good for military history, it is less clear that the controversy this section exam-ines has been as productive or beneficial. The controversy concerns a set of ideas that are characterized by the notions of western exceptionalism – the idea that Western Europe has followed a notably different path of historical development from the rest of the world, with "different" often equated with "better" – and dominance or superiority, but that are probably better known in both popular and academic history under the heading "The Western Way of War," the title of the book by Victor Davis Hanson that generated the controversy in its modern form.

In some ways the idea of western superiority is as old as the modern historical profession, for it was a central tenet of nineteenth-century European (and US) historical writing that Europe possessed the most advanced races, civilization, and military systems in the world. And at least in terms of military force, they were arguably correct. Late nineteenth-century European armies, supplied by industry, moved by steam power, and organized by powerful, rich administrations, clearly outclassed the armed forces available to any other state. Even formerly powerful empires such as the Ottomans fell far behind European military might; the only state outside Europe to join the ranks of great powers in the nineteenth century, Japan, did so by adopting western industrial and military organization lock, stock, and barrel. The deeply ingrained racist attitudes about European superiority that accompanied and reinforced colonialism permeated historical writing, so that western exceptionalism through the mid-twentieth century was not a controversy but an assumed fact. The trend since the 1960s, however, has been to question, deconstruct, and distrust any such claims as Eurocentric, potentially racist, and misleading about the dynamics of the past. The rise of world history since the late 1980s has emphasized that trend. Resistance to the decentering of the West in historical terms has come mostly in the form of defense of an intellectual notion of a "western tradition" that informs educational agendas. This has been a clearly political split, with conservatives on the side of defending an idea of western exceptionalism, though one more carefully defined and circumscribed than the nineteenth-century version.

Hanson, an historian of classical Greece, began to build an expanded defense of western exceptionalism and, crucially, superiority, in a 1989 book entitled *The Western Way of War. Infantry Battle in Classical Greece.*[18] The subtitle actually described the true focus of the work: this was a Keegan-inspired "face of battle" examination of what hoplite phalanx battles were like for those who engaged in them (Keegan in fact wrote the introduction). On those terms, it succeeded brilliantly. And Hanson, a California farmer as well as an academic, offered an interpretation of Greek warfare that questioned the accepted picture of phalanxes fighting to protect their city-state's cropland: his experience was that the key Greek crops, olives and grapes, would in fact have been very difficult for a small infantry army to damage seriously. Rather, phalanx battles arose out of an implicit cultural agreement among Greek city-states that face-to-face battle was the way to settle disputes. That cultural agreement was intimately associated with a connection between civic and military duty that was central to Greek life.

Though Hanson's conclusions about Greek tactics, strategy, and especially the development of "civic militarism" have been questioned by other Greek specialists,[19] these are the sorts of disagreements common among specialists in every field. What attracted much wider attention and dispute was the claim Hanson built on his examination of Greek hoplite warfare: that the Greeks had established a "western way of war" characterized by face-to-face shock combat (as opposed to the more indirect and missile-oriented tactics of "oriental" warfare) and supported by political-military systems built on citizenship (as opposed to subjection) and a resulting "civic militarism." This style, he claimed, remained a constant characteristic of western combat and led to the triumph of western civilization globally. Though he only sketched these claims in *The Western Way of War*, Hanson has subsequently focused on and elaborated them in a series of provocatively titled books, including *Why the West Has Won: Nine Landmark Battles in the Brutal History of Western Victory* and *Carnage and Culture: Landmark Battles in the Rise of Western Power*.[20]

Some scholars have taken on Hanson's argument at this larger level. John Lynn's book *Battle: A History of Combat and Culture*[21] is among the most extended and telling critiques. And Hanson has found support at least for some aspects of his account: a version of his argument runs through the *Cambridge Illustrated History of Warfare*,[22] to which Hanson contributed chapters on Greece and Rome. But a number of military historians have refused to engage with Hanson's thesis directly because of what they see as his increasingly polemical tone, the overtly political intent of his works (they are often promoted through right-wing media), and what they see as the scholarly weakness of his argument. Setting aside the political aspect of these reactions, what philosophical and methodological issues do Hanson's argument and the responses it has drawn raise?

The first issue is how does one define "the West." It is not a geographic designation (except in the broadest sense, in that it derives from the fact that Europe is the westernmost peninsula of Asia), because Hanson counts Rome as the "western" power in its wars with Carthage. Carthage is, of course, west of Rome. On the other hand, neither do some forms of administrative and cultural continuity count, for Byzantium, the direct heir of Rome, seems not to make in onto the list of "western" powers. Perhaps this is because Byzantium "lost," having been extinguished by the Ottoman Turks in 1453. For the key to being "western" in Hanson's schema seems to be "coming out a winner by the nineteenth century," which means Western European powers and the US (along with their spiritual ancestors) are the sole qualifiers. Equally problematic, and implied in who counts as "western," is the question of what defines "non-western" powers. Given that Hanson's argument portrays non-western powers as unstable, despotic, and ineffective, one fundamental premise of the project risks committing "orientalism," to use Edward Said's term for the tendency for European and American writers to both amalgamate and denigrate the historical experiences of non-Europeans.[23] It is certainly true that Hanson avoids the sort of careful comparative analysis of different societies, especially non-western ones, that feature in, for instance, Geoffrey Parker's analysis of China in *The Military Revolution*. In other words, unlike Parker, Hanson does not contribute to the globalization of military history.

The problem of defining "the West" extends to what counts today as "western," a problem highlighted in the triumphalism of his book titles. Claiming that "the West has won" not only commits the presentist error of assuming that history has ended in terms of this question, but also conflates "modern" with "western." (In other words, is a Japan or, potentially, China outfitted with modern military equipment and the mechanisms of mass participatory politics then automatically a "western" power? Or do modern (industrial) polities and cultures come in as many varieties as did premodern (pre-industrial) cultures, with all of them modern but only some of them western?)

That Greece and Rome qualify only as "spiritual ancestors" of modern western powers is a conclusion that necessarily emerges not just from Hanson's omission of Byzantium from the list of western powers, but from the major substantive problem military historians find with Hanson's thesis: the place of the Middle Ages in his argument. Or more accurately, its lack of a place. Hanson posits the Greeks as the creators of a continuous, connected tradition of civic militarism that made western powers more effective militarily – "more effective killers" – than their rivals. But no historian of Imperial Rome or of medieval military history would accept Hanson's characterization of western "civic militarism" as applying to the Roman Empire or medieval Western Europe, nor would the history of Western European military conflict between 400 and 1400 supply much support for the superiority of a "western way of war." (Indeed, the military superpower of that period, the Mongols, might well be the best example of "civic militarism" one could find, in that Mongol tribal organization included all free males as part of the political-military community and was organized for bloody, effective warfare. But the Mongols are the antithesis of the agrarianism that Hanson places at the foundations of Greek civic militarism, and their credentials as a "western" power are therefore fatally flawed, for this and numerous other obvious reasons.) Without continuity between classical Greece and the modern West, Hanson's argument loses much of its force.

Finally, the consistent superiority for the "western way of war" that Hanson claims is open to question. The Mongols and other steppe nomadic peoples were, as noted above, probably the most effective armies in the world for several millennia down to the seventeenth century. The careful comparative studies of Jeremy Black, John Lynn, and others show that western armies had no advantage over those of other settled societies (never mind the nomads) until perhaps the drilled armies of the eighteenth century, and that the global extension of European power in the nineteenth century depended crucially on a range of factors, many of which were non-military. Yes, European armies could deploy steam-powered gunboats, rifled muskets, and later machine guns. But they also deployed the vast economic and organizational advantages that came from industrialization, the tools of scientific medicine, and a demographic advantage derived from both of these (the proportion of people globally with European ancestry in 1900 was higher than it ever had been, and has declined steadily ever since). The record of conventional, "western"-style armies against unconventional forces, including Mao Zedong's Chinese Communists, colonial rebels, and terrorists in the twentieth century, is not exactly a record of unbroken success. Indeed, it is odd that one of the battles Hanson highlights in *Carnage and Culture* is the Tet Offensive of 1968, which while indeed a tactical victory for US forces over the North Vietnamese, doomed the US war effort because of its effect on popular support for the war – and western civic militarism is, according to Hanson, supposed to produce more determined cultural support for war than autocratic non-western states can muster. And calling all the armies that opposed such forces (and each other) "western" overlooks the significant organizational and cultural differences that separate modern armies such as the Red Army of the USSR, the Wehrmacht of Nazi Germany, and the US army, differences that show up in variations of doctrinal approach to battle.[24]

Like the debate about military revolutions, the controversy over a "western way of war" has subsumed some older topics of discussion among military historians, recasting their issues in its own terms. In particular, questions about the true extent of European military superiority have informed studies of nineteenth- and twentieth-century colonial warfare, especially the costs and difficulties of western resistance to decolonization. The basic dynamic here pits the one-sided, triumphalist narratives of traditional western historiography against the attempts of postcolonial theorists to introduce, through subaltern studies, the voice and agency of the colonized in the history of colonialism. In military terms, this can play out, for example, in more nuanced cultural analyses of the formation and effectiveness of the sepoy regiments – soldiers drawn from the colonized peoples (especially in India, whence the term originates) but trained in western military methods. Studies have argued both that the effectiveness of British sepoy organization derived from the way the British embedded regimental organization in Indian caste and religious differences, and conversely that, like contemporary European regiments, sepoy regimental culture became something separate from civil society.[25] What is clear from all such studies is the importance of culture in shaping the ways in which peoples fight and how unconventional wars are won. Much of the relevance of new examinations of colonial warfare has to do, in fact, with the problems of fighting terrorism specifically and unconventional wars generally. As a result, the "western way of war" debate also tends to merge with the wider, not necessarily military, historiography of "clashes of civilization," as in Thomas P. M. Barnett's *The Pentagon's New Map.*[26]

While the historiography of colonial and unconventional warfare is opening fertile new fields for exploration, and the emphasis in Hanson's work on a western "culture of war" has stimulated the general cultural turn in military history, the overall impact of the "western way of war" debate is, arguably, much more mixed than that of the military revolution debates. While it is true that all historians have a perspective – a set of current interests that shape their questions about the past – Hanson's overtly political intent and polemical tone have struck some as shifting the balance too far toward presentism and away from understanding the past on its own terms, and indeed threatening to distort our understanding of the past. More generally, the "back to the nineteenth century" quality of the project – the emphases on western superiority, decisive battles, and so forth – while successful with segments of the popular audience for military history, has not had the same effect as the military revolution debate in helping move military history further into the mainstream of globalizing, culturally oriented, contemporary historiography.

War, Society, and Culture:
Other Controversies

Rather than focusing on one large controversy, as the last two sections have done, this section will examine more briefly a representative set of more limited topics of contention in military history. These include arguments that revolve around the relationship of war, society, and culture, as well as more traditional arguments about the features of military operations themselves, though even here the new perspectives brought to the field by social and cultural history have had an influence. An indication of the new directions in which military history is headed is provided by the fact that the interaction of war-making and culture, especially the interaction between idealized notions of how war should be fought (often instantiated in the cultures and values of warrior elites, values that at times have assumed more or less formalized form as "warrior codes") and the actual practice of warfare has been examined in theoretically explicit ways. Specifically, John Lynn has developed a model of the process of interaction that should provide a fine starting point for further analysis of such topics.[27] The set of discussions that follow attempt to sample controversies from a broad sweep of military history, and are arranged in chronological order.

Roman continuity?

Military historians of the early Middle Ages (roughly the period from the break-up of the western Roman Empire in the mid-fifth century to the recognizable beginnings of a new era in the mid-tenth century) are currently divided into two major camps with regard to the nature of early medieval warfare. Their different interpretations of the period are an excellent example of how military history is necessarily inextricable from broader social, economic, and political developments, and also illustrate the impact of new sorts of sources on the state of knowledge in a field.

On one side is a group of historians who see continuity from late Roman times as the central characteristic of the period. In other words, they see Roman military organization, training, strategic and tactical principles, and patterns of campaigning as pervasive throughout the early medieval world. They furthermore build this military picture on a view of economic and administrative continuity: that Roman levels of economic activity continued through the period with no demographic decline, that kingdoms deployed the written word constantly and maintained functioning bureaucracies, and that warfare was essentially a tool of statecraft conducted by big armies.[28] On the other side is a group of historians who see much more transformation. Starting from evidence of significant demographic and economic decline, they argue that the character of armed forces evolved rapidly away from Roman state-based models. They trace a process that began with the construction of barbarian ethnic identities around the right to bear arms, and eventuated in the rise of socially dominant military aristocracies at the expense of state power. Their view of strategy, tactics, and the cultural expressions of warfare and military privilege stress both simplified modes of combat, greater social embeddedness, and much smaller numbers in armies.[29]

The issues of interpretation involved are complex. The language of the sources, at least on the surface, supports the Roman continuity view, as Roman terms remain in use throughout the period. But careful reading of the sources in the light of other evidence – especially archaeological findings relating to demographic and economic conditions, as well as weapons caches in burial sites, whose cultural implications are illuminated by anthropological theory and comparison – show how misleading naive readings of the sources can be.[30] The argument also tends to pit philosophical universalists on the continuity side against social constructionists on the transformation side. The centrality of socio-military developments to interpretation of the entire period is such that this controversy extends well beyond the bounds of strictly military history. It is safe to say that though the debate is vigorous and at times heated, the preponderance of opinion among early medieval specialists certainly lies with those arguing transformation, small numbers, and a backdrop of demographic and economic decline.[31] Their position is supported also by comparison with less contentious interpretations of Byzantine and Arab warfare during the same period (though there are a few Roman maximalists who argue for large numbers in Byzantine armies as well).[32]

In historiographical terms, this debate has largely superseded an earlier one, now largely settled among medieval military historians, about feudalism – or more accurately, about the lack of such a thing. Though still sometimes seen in popular accounts or some textbooks as the typical medieval mode of military organization, "feudalism" (whose lack of precise meaning is one of its central problems) is a construct that has basically been abandoned by specialists in medieval military history except in very constrained cases, that usually date to the later Middle Ages. The technological determinist argument that feudalism originated with the introduction of the stirrup and a consequent rise in the effectiveness of mounted shock combat has been thoroughly discredited, and the whole notion of a "feudal society" is in question, while analysis of land-for-service arrangements are moving to a broader, comparative basis that tries to avoid the shoehorning of evidence necessary when "feudal" structures are assumed as a starting point for analyzing such military manpower systems.[33] To the extent that the socio-military structures that used to be characterized as "feudal" originated in the early Middle Ages, those origins are now conceptualized in terms set by the debate over Roman (dis)continuity.

Giving up the gun?

The fate of gunpowder weaponry in Tokugawa Japan (1600–1868) provides an interesting case study in contrasting interpretations of an historical episode where the "facts" are much better known than in early medieval Europe, where basic evidence is often limited and obscure. The "problem" to be explained here is not disputed. More than a century of intense warfare (1477–1600) between the small rival states that made up Japan at the time resulted in the loose unification of the islands under Tokugawa Ieyasu. During the period of warfare, gunpowder weapons had appeared in Japan in 1543, brought by a Portuguese trading ship. Within a short period of time, Japanese smiths were forging muskets the equal of those

NOT LINEAR

anywhere, and Japanese commanders, especially the innovative Oda Nobunaga, were making effective tactical use of musketry in combination with bow fire and massed spear formations. Nobunaga may, in fact, have invented volley fire before Maurice of Nassau came up with the technique in Europe. Yet within 45 years of Tokugawa Ieyasu's decisive victory over his rivals in 1601, his successor as Shogun (military ruler of Japan) had suppressed the internal manufacturing of gunpowder weapons (cannon as well as muskets), banned foreign trade not just in weaponry but almost completely, and encouraged the rise of a "Cult of the Sword" among the samurai who now made up the military ruling class of the country. The spontaneous abandonment of an effective, superior military technology is a relatively rare and surprising event in the annals of military history, and the parallels up to that point between military evolution in Japan and in Western Europe, where the cumulative developments of weaponry and technique were significant enough to inspire the idea of a military revolution among historians (as we detailed above), makes the Japanese decision all the more interesting. How to explain it?

The most popular current explanation is cultural: the antipathy of Japanese warriors to guns was such that they rejected the technology to affirm their cultural identity, in effect. The most effective presentation of this argument is by Noel Perrin, whose book *Giving Up the Gun*[34] gives this section its subtitle. The cultural argument has been taken up prominently by John Keegan in his *History of Warfare*, where the Japanese resistance to gunpowder weapons is compared to an apparently similar antipathy among the Mamluks who ruled Egypt in the fifteenth century and who eventually lost power to the Ottoman Turks, who were willing to adopt guns. Part of the popularity of Perrin's thesis among academics may derive from the lesson that he explicitly draws from it: that it is possible for a culture to decide to reject effective weapons, and that the Japanese experience with guns provides a model for attitudes toward nuclear weapons.

But an alternative explanation, while not rejecting culture as a factor in the reception of military technology, disputes the independent power of culture in Tokugawa Japan's abandonment of guns. This explanation stresses the potentially disruptive nature of hand guns, which are relatively easy to manufacture in large numbers and may be deployed effectively by unskilled troops with only a minimum of training. The Tokugawa settlement after a century of internal warfare was politically a fragile affair built not on hegemonic conquest by the Tokugawa house but on a set of alliances that created a federal-style system. The political settlement went hand-in-hand with a social settlement that froze the fluid and relatively mobile class structure of the previous period into a rigid caste system backed by Confucian ideology, with the samurai at the top, and granted a monopoly on the right to carry weapons and use force. In this context, suppressing gunpowder weapons looks less like an idealizing cultural move and more like the most effective way for a small ruling elite to stabilize the state and prevent civil unrest. It is of a piece, in this view, with the related policies of closing off foreign contact and persecuting the sizable population of Japanese Christian converts who, the leaders of the Shogunate assumed, owed divided allegiance to a foreign lord (the Pope).[35] This dispute again shows how interpretation of military events is usually intimately tied up with the entire historical development of a society, and that the same evidence can admit of different and competing explanations, neither of which is implausible on the face of it.

The origins of blitzkrieg

World War II, Hitler, and the Nazis are a perennially hot topic in military history publishing.[36] Much of this volume of publication consists of popular syntheses and "niche market" examinations of small pieces of the larger picture, which is not to say that new interpretations and quality research cannot emerge in such venues. (The same characterization could also apply to that other staple of US military history publishing, the American Civil War.) But an ongoing controversy within that subfield is worth examining here, as it demonstrates not just interesting aspects of how academic historians argue with each other and how even the most traditionally military topics are now set in social and cultural contexts, but that such arguments can have real resonance within professional military circles as well. That controversy concerns the origins and nature of "blitzkrieg," the popular name for the operational doctrine and techniques of the German Wehrmacht in World War II, whose stunning successes, especially in the opening phases of the war, still hold the promise of lessons in decisive campaigning for contemporary armed forces.

Unlike the deep and heated bipolar division that characterizes the argument over Roman continuity, the arguments over blitzkrieg are more multifaceted and less fundamental. Almost every historian involved in the debate agrees, for instance, that the evolution of blitzkrieg doctrine was not the "natural" and inevitable result of the introduction of new technologies – that is, this is an explicitly anti-technological determinist debate. Rather, the arguments concern the balance among a variety of generally agreed-on factors. Was blitzkrieg generated more from within the German doctrinal tradition, adapting new technology to operational doctrine and a strategic context with roots as deep as Frederick the Great?[37] Or did 1920s British armor doctrine, especially the writings of J. F. C. Fuller and B. H. Liddell Hart, form fundamental influences adopted by the German General Staff, with the impetus for radical change provided by defeat in World War I?[38] Was Heinz Guderian the individual creative genius who invented blitzkrieg and forced it on a reluctant General Staff?[39] Or was there widespread support for the idea of mechanized and armored units even before Guderian assumed command, with a number of German thinkers (drawing on British ideas?), including Hans von Seeckt, contributing key concepts?[40] The similarity between the Wehrmacht's blitzkrieg doctrine and the Soviet "deep battle" doctrine developed up to 1936 but abandoned in Stalin's purges (only to be revived after the Nazi invasion of 1941) has led scholars to question the possible mutual influences between the Wehrmacht and the Red Army, especially given their secret joint exercises conducted in the 1920s. Was this purely German influence on the Soviets,[41] mutual influence, the influence on both of British writers, or convergent evolution under similar cultural, strategic, and doctrinal conditions and assumptions?[42] While a number of these options can look like mutually exclusive dichotomies, in practice many of the historians involved differ only in the weight they assign to each factor, stressing that while, for example, there may have been opposition to some of Guderian's ideas, this opposition was more in the nature of a moderating influence than obstructionism, and coexisted with support among many members of the General Staff for the basic concepts.

The history of the development of blitzkrieg warfare is part of a larger history of interwar doctrinal ferment that included fierce disputes within various national armed forces about the effectiveness and uses of airpower, especially strategic bombing, and naval technology (which of course included the impact of airpower and the relative merits of battleships and aircraft carriers). As in some of these other cases, the congruence between doctrine and reality, between theory and practice, has also been a matter of dispute, as historians and military professionals alike attempt to understand not just the idea of blitzkrieg, but also how it played out in actual campaigns. While few historians take positions as extreme as that which claims that the whole idea of blitzkrieg is a myth,[43] some have pointed out that the initial German victories in Poland and France that gave blitzkrieg its reputation did not in fact instantiate the doctrine very well (or contributed substantially to its ongoing development by highlighting problems),[44] and many emphasize its inherent limitations, especially the logistical difficulties it imposes on armies attempting to implement it over large distances and the difficult challenges of command and control that it poses.[45] Robert Citino's multi-volume study of operational warfare in the twentieth century is particularly impressive for how he ties the differing implementations of the fundamental concepts of mobile warfare to different national strategic situations and cultures – pointing out, for instance, that despite some surface similarities, Soviet "deep battle" and Wehrmacht blitzkrieg differed significantly in practice because of very different assumptions on the part of German and Russian leaders about how valuable and replaceable manpower was.

Conclusion: Revisionism and Reading the Process of History

The debate over the development and implementation of blitzkrieg doctrine, with its multifaceted issues, lack of clear polarities, and new positions built around a core of rough agreement about the issues, is in fact fairly typical of how historical study progresses. Vast ideological disagreements are rare, and most academic historians are cautious creatures whose favorite phrase is often "the truth lies somewhere in the middle." New understandings often complement rather than contradict older notions, and even if they do challenge received wisdom may enter the historiographical stage without meeting much resistance. Geoffrey Wawro's brilliant narrative of the Franco-Prussian War, for example, revisits the strategy and tactics of the war in light of new archival research and brings the personal, "face of battle" sensibility to bear on the experience of war; it thus mostly updates Michael Howard's older account of the war, improving our understanding of it incrementally without necessarily discrediting Howard's interpretation.[46] When it does depart significantly from received wisdom, it is to suggest that the German Chancellor Otto von Bismarck became carried away during the difficult endgame of the war, letting emotion lead him away from the limited aims with which he started the conflict to dictate a peace settlement that laid the seeds for future conflict. Wawro's *Franco-Prussian War* therefore becomes part of an ongoing debate about the causes of World War I. In that debate, undoubtedly the most controversial and interesting book to come out on the subject in many years is Niall Ferguson's *The Pity of War*,[47] which argues that Britain should not have intervened in 1914: the costs were far too high for the benefits received. Ferguson's interpretation of World War I comes from the perspective of an economic historian and depends on a fascinating use of counterfactual history, the technique of imagining alternative historical paths to highlight contingent features of the path the world actually followed. (Counterfactual history tends to be associated with economic history, whose deep trends and theoretical grounding in economics seem to suggest different possible outcomes more than other approaches to history often do.)

Such interlocked debates, constant revisions of the commonly accepted picture of the past, and new interpretations constitute the bulk of what historians do in any field, and military history is no different. The range of controversies sketched here, from large and philosophically fundamental to more restricted and merely representative, do show military history to be a vital and changing piece of the larger historical profession, for a field of history without some deep divisions and ongoing arguments is ready to lie fallow. In military history, many different crops are still springing from the soil of historical evidence fertilized by new theoretical and methodological approaches, and this rough guide to current controversies can be neither complete nor remain current. Students exploring new work in these fields or work in other areas of military history can usually figure out where a book they are reading falls with respect to previous work by paying attention to the book's preface or introduction. Historians usually provide their own historiographical context in one of these places in order to point out how what they are doing is new, innovative, or otherwise noteworthy. Careful reading of these historiographical introductions, informed by knowledge of the basic philosophical, methodological, and historiographical contours of military history that this book tries to provide, should allow students to explore new fields of military history more effectively.

5
Doing Military History

As we have seen already, military history has long existed not just in the form of an academic field of study, but also as a form of popular literature and as a branch of professional military education. While each of these branches of military history is distinct, having somewhat different audiences and therefore somewhat different goals, they certainly overlap to some extent. Furthermore, they share certain deeper bonds that apply to any historical research: practical questions about form of presentation, access to and interpretation of sources, and so on. This chapter will survey some of these major practical questions about doing military history. We will first consider the various forms that military history takes (or that partake of the expertise of military historians); unlike the emphasis of previous chapters on academic writing, our attention will here be spread to other media. The next section will examine the sources for military history, sources common to military history in any form. This will lead to a survey of the places where programs in military history exist, bringing us back to a focus on academic military history. With this focus, the last section discusses the major publishing outlets for military scholarship.

Forms

Military history today appears in many different media in addition to the traditional published formats – books and articles. Even written military history may show up on the world wide web in more or less formally "published" form, while history on television, in movies, in conjunction with battlefield tours at National Parks, and in the form of historical recreations is increasingly common. Before analyzing the implications of such different forms, however, a more fundamental problem about form faces historians working in any of these media. As in any field of history, military historians face a choice between narrative exposition and thematic analysis. That is, history tells a story about some aspect of the past. But simply recounting a series of events or retelling a story from a primary source barely qualifies as history: such writing is analogous to collecting ancient artifacts with no attempt to understand what they tell us about past times. A narrative without analysis, in other words, risks becoming antiquarianism, the display of disconnected pieces of the past for curiosity value. The job of the historian is to analyze his sources for what they say about bigger themes, not just display them. On the other hand, thematic analysis without a story about the past isn't history either. Historians must do both, balancing the sometimes conflicting demands of narrative and thematic analysis, of telling a story and highlighting the inner characteristics of the story.

Depending partly on the subject, the balance can vary. Some historians emphasize the narrative structure of their work, embedding the analysis in the narrative (or even holding analysis until after the story is over). Geoffrey Wawro's *Franco-Prussian War*, noted in the last chapter, does an excellent job of weaving analysis of strategy, tactics, and the political, social, economic and diplomatic contexts of the war into an essentially narrative format that tells the story of the war from beginning to end. Others arrange their presentation according to the demands of the theme. John France's masterly *Western Warfare in the Age of the Crusades, 1000–1300*[1] weaves numerous small narratives from the sources into chapters built around themes: war, society, and technology;

weapons of war; the relationship of warfare and property holding; and so forth. Another interesting way of analyzing a particular war thematically rather than through a chronological narrative appears in Victor Davis Hanson's *A War Like no Other: How the Athenians and Spartans Fought the Peloponnesian War*,[2] which approaches this mutigenerational conflict through the lens of types of conflict.

Another way of putting this tension is that historians must accomplish two seemingly contradictory tasks: first, presenting a picture of some piece of the past at a moment in time, for which purpose thematic analysis is often well suited; and second, explaining change over time, which implies (though does not require) a narrative exposition (though telling about change and explaining it are different things). While all historians must decide what balance best suits their chosen subject, the strong pull of "story" inherent in military operations, with their tendency to produce winners and losers, has traditionally pulled most military histories toward narrative structures – a tendency not unrelated to the prevalence of Great Man theory and Decisive Battle morality in traditional military history. But this has been balanced in recent decades by the tendencies of social and cultural history toward thematic analysis, a tendency necessitated by the focus of these disciplines on common people and mass experience that can only be accessed by extracting themes from a mass of tiny narrative fragments.

The challenge of presenting both narrative and theme exists for historians working in media other than the written word, and the balance between the two can be affected by the medium. Television, for example, which excels at showing individual people and visually compelling stories (and especially at telling short, segmented stories), is probably inherently biased toward narrative and against deep, thematically based analysis. In this, it coincides with the traditional tendencies of military history just noted. It should therefore probably not be surprising that much of the programming of the History Channel is either military history or biography. The tendency toward story is even stronger in movies, which cannot even extend treatment of a subject over a series or season. Much history in the movies thus remains essentially costume drama, though digital technology can now create far more complex, detailed and at least potentially accurate settings for toga stories (the visual depictions of Rome in *Gladiator* come to mind, balanced by the bizarre fantasy city of *Troy*). The web as a medium, however, with its non-linear structure and hyperlinks, seems potentially even better suited for thematic analysis than printed books, though assessment of its possibilities must at this stage remain tentative due to the relative novelty of the medium.

The great advantage of "publishing" military history on the web is the degree of control over the final product that it affords the historian. No one else – publisher, editor, reviewers – need have any input into web publishing, and in the form of blogs needn't even be all that polished. Such web publishing can be a quick way to get feedback from a wide audience and to publicize collaborative projects. The corresponding danger, of course, is that there is no quality assurance for web publishing of the sort that peer-reviewed print publishing provides. There is peer-reviewed web publishing (much more prevalent at the moment in scientific fields than in humanities), and the student or researcher is responsible for evaluating the reliability of information obtained from websites. This is obviously true of any source of information; it is just that the quantity of information easily accessible on the web makes it more problematic in this regard. It is by giving up some control over the final product to editors and pre-publication reviewers that an author can put a sort of preliminary seal of approval on the work, showing that it at least meets basic academic standards (though academic dishonesty in the form of plagiarism can still slip through). Scholarly publications – academic journals and books from university presses – are in this respect usually even more rigorous than large market commercial presses, whose "trade books" are evaluated on sales potential as much as academic quality.

Military historians who work on television and movie productions almost always give up even more control over the final product. An historical TV series written and hosted by a prominent historian retains the most control, but must craft the text to the medium and leave the production of the visual product to a crew. Historians who act as "talking heads" on historical TV series can help shape the finished product, but rarely have final say over the script. Historians acting as advisors on movies have the least control, and must sometimes accept that their input will be ignored in favor of entertainment value. And of course much advice about the recreation of battle scenes has long been subject to the limitations of available manpower: Stanley Kubrick was able to stage a fairly large Roman legionary formation in *Spartacus* with the help not only of historical advisors but of 8,000 infantrymen of the Spanish army who served as extras. (If the manpower is available, however, the movie set can become a site for "experimental archaeology" of a sort: one specialist in eighteenth-century warfare gained a first-hand appreciation for the difficulty of maintaining a dressed line of infantry in an advance over broken terrain by acting as the commanding officer for such a formation in a movie.)

Recreation of battles for movies shades into another form that military history takes: historical re-enactment. Some re-enactments are, naturally, less serious than others. "Renaissance Faires" and some other medieval re-enactments owe more to Arthurian fantasy than to historical research; one is sometimes tempted to ask "Where are the peasants? Who has died of plague recently?" But serious armor and weapons recreation can add significantly to scholarly knowledge. And some groups, notably many American Civil War re-enactment societies, are composed, in effect, of a democratic group of social historians whose attention to details of everyday life (clothing, food, household technology) is impressive and well researched. Some members of such groups, especially those portraying Confederate soldiers, even put themselves on very restricted (and authentic) diets to achieve the proper emaciated-from-inadequate-logistical-support look. It is interesting that the most authentic and popular historical re-enactment groups all work in the "civil war" genre: Japanese re-enactors focus on the *sengoku jidai*, the sixteenth-century age of warring diamyo domains that ended in the Tokugawa unification; English re-enactors refight the musket-and-pike battles from the English Civil War of the mid-seventeenth century; and then there are the American Civil War groups just mentioned. American Revolution re-enacting is also quite popular, and it too has something of the character of a civil war. Exploration of the cultural dynamics and implications for "historical memory" of this phenomenon is probably worth someone's research project. Perhaps the best example of re-enactors supporting more scholarly inquiry into a particular area is the Roman Military Equipment Conference. This biennial conference brings together archaeologists, art historians, classicists, and military historians with re-enactors in an effort to look at Roman military equipment in all of its contexts: archaeological (traditional and experimental), artistic, and literary.

Returning to movie recreations of battles, manpower restrictions no longer apply when battle choreographers can work with digitally generated soldiers, as for instance with the computer program Massive used by Peter Jackson to make the battle scenes in *Lord of the Rings*. But the potential of such programs – and of their commercial kin, computer simulations of warfare such as *Medieval Total War* – for research into war and as venues for the publication of serious inquiry into the nature of battle has so far been very limited, as game designers and fantasy imagery have until now dominated their development. (Jackson could have used a military historian to tell him that no cavalry troop in any world could charge down a hill as steep as the one Gandalf charged down at Helm's Deep, and in fact Tolkien wrote that attack as an infantry charge.) In this respect, computer games are still catching up with military simulation board games, whose popularity and historical authenticity both peaked in the late 1970s and early 1980s, just before the rise of personal computers. Simulations Publications Inc. (SPI), no longer extant, was the most historically conscientious. In short, gaming remains an underdeveloped form for research and publishing in serious military history, but one with interesting potential, for if properly constrained, the ability to replay "the story" with different outcomes – to explore counterfactual history – can actually highlight recurring themes, wedding narrative to analysis.

Sources

The constraint on replaying an historical episode in a game or, more traditionally, on the presentation and interpretation of the past in written and other forms, comes ultimately from the sources themselves. For unlike fantasy (where horses assisted by digital magic can charge down steep hills), history should conform to the realities of the physical world and to the more restrictive and contentious evidence left to us of past events. What are the sources for military history? The discussion here will be restricted to *primary sources*, that is, sources from the time of the events being studied, the raw material of history, as opposed to *secondary sources*, or modern historical interpretations. ("Primary" and "secondary" do *not* refer to the importance of a source for a particular problem.) The distinction is not always clear cut, of course. Livy, despite living several hundred years after the early Republican period of Roman history, is still about as close as we can get to a primary source for that period. Gibbon's *Decline and Fall of the Roman Empire*, however, despite having been written more than 200 years ago, is nevertheless a secondary source for the history of Rome. It could be a primary source, however, for an intellectual history of the eighteenth century.

We may consider the sources for military history (which naturally share much in common with the sources for other sorts of history) from several different angles. First, where are sources to be found? The basic division is between unpublished and published sources. Unpublished sources exist mostly in archives of one sort or another, and research in archives is usually part of the initiation into the academic historical profession. Governments, universities, and museums (often state-supported) are the usual keepers of archives, but valuable collections can be found in the archives of other institutions, from medieval monasteries to modern newspapers, and these days include not just paper (or parchment, papyrus rolls, stone tablets, and so forth) but microfilm and digital archives.

Primary sources may be published in a variety of ways: in traditional print form, on CD-ROMs (as, for example, a fine digital version of the Bayeux Tapestry[3] or the massive Official Records of the War of the Rebellion for the American Civil War), or on the web. Publication of a source usually takes either or both of two forms: an *edition*, in which a scholar produces a print version in the original language of a manuscript or archival source, preferably with annotations as to uncertain readings, possible scribal errors, and gaps in the source, or indeed notes about what parts of the source the editor has chosen not to include; and a *translation* of the source into a modern language, if necessary, or into English from another modern language (from the parochial American point of view). Editions can of course vary in quality, and with ancient or medieval sources are ideally produced from multiple manuscript copies in order to check for scribal errors. The more potentially problematic issue, especially for military historians, is with translations. Few translations are done by specifically military historians, and then only of key texts that are obviously military in character. But in most places and times, military information must be gleaned from sources whose main original and modern audiences will have different interests. The nuances of technical military terminology may not survive non-specialist translations. Even apparently simple military terms in other languages that may be translated by such simple words as "soldier," "infantry," and "cavalry" may hide important military information. The Latin word *miles*, for example, means "soldier" (sometimes with the connotation "elite, well-armed soldier") in a classical context, and so usually refers to the infantry of the Roman legions. But by the twelfth century, the same precise meaning remained but now usually referred to the armored horsemen who dominated medieval society and warfare. Its secondary meaning has therefore shifted to "cavalry" instead of "infantry" and in fact it has come to be commonly (and often misleadingly) translated as "knight."[4] Interpretations of military developments can, in other words, be hidden in and influenced by source translations, a problem of which both student and professional historians must be aware.

A second categorization of sources is by type. Here, the sorts of sources historians wish to use will depend partly on the sorts of history they intend to write. Given that military activity is often (though certainly not exclusively) a state-sponsored activity, official government documents such as payroll rosters, muster lists, tables of organization, operational orders, and so on are valuable.[5] The problem is that they exist, especially in usable runs, only for very restricted places and times, with Western Europe maintaining an unusually full documentation of its past since about the fourteenth century. Such documentation increases further with an explosion of official military archives since the nineteenth century, when the US also began keeping copious records. Thus, more general histories and chronicles of the sort discussed in chapter 2 are almost always crucial. Where possible, more personal records – memoirs, common soldiers' letters home, diaries – provide wonderful windows into the experience of warfare, a view sometimes provided by literary forms such as poetry in societies without the tools of widespread personal literacy. Of course, many societies have been largely illiterate, even when writing was a tool of elites, and many wartime experiences, even in societies with mass literacy, never get written down. Oral history, whether in the (written and complicated) form recorded in oral epic poetry or as interviews with soldiers conducted by professional historians, is therefore not just useful but necessary if historians wish to access the full range of military experience, though the limits of oral sources are also obvious. Finally, material sources are essential to military history. Nothing beats walking around a battlefield, castle, or fortification for getting an idea of the parameters of physical reality in warfare, while weapons, armor, pictorial representations of warfare, and so forth act as a vital check on and supplement to written sources.

Finally, whatever the type or location of source, there are issues of source criticism that are common to every historical field and so lie largely beyond a survey focused on military history. Written and pictorial sources have their own perspectives and biases that must be accounted for, and even material remains come from a context that can crucially affect how they should be interpreted. Some sources are more reliable than others. Careful evaluation of one's sources is the first responsibility of any historian.

Programs

There are military historians and historians with military interests scattered through colleges and universities across the world. But programs in military history are much more rare, particularly at the graduate level. Military history programs come in two varieties, related to the types of military history we have identified throughout this book. The first type consists of programs aimed at professional military education (PME), chiefly those programs at national service academies, including Sandhurst, West Point, Annapolis, and the Air Force Academy, as well as advanced service schools, aimed at continuing professional education and development for military officers, such as the Naval, Army, and Air War Colleges and the various Command and Staff Colleges. The academies are undergraduate institutions, and vary in how closely their organization resembles civilian universities – the faculty at the US Naval Academy at Annapolis is organized much more along civilian academic lines, for instance, than the one at West Point. The Command and Staff Colleges and War Colleges are graduate institutions and tend to be organized differently – more akin to research institutes and centers in civilian institutions – although some, like the Naval War College, do offer graduate degrees.

The second type consists of academic programs that grant graduate degrees in military history. Academic programs and institutional specializations tend to change over time, so the source most guaranteed to be up-to-date is the online guide to graduate programs in military history maintained by the Society for Military History (see next section).[6] Some of these programs offer only a Master's degree, some offer PhDs. The best-known PhD programs with significant concentrations in military history are at Ohio State University, Temple University, and Duke University, which runs a program with connections to the University of North Carolina at Chapel Hill. Although concentrated mostly in the US, there are also programs in England and Canada. It is also possible, of course, to do a PhD in a military subject at a university that does not run a program in military history. The job of prospective students in such cases is to identify a scholar whose work seems related to their interest, find where the scholar teaches, and (assuming it is a place that has graduate programs in history) apply to that history graduate program, specifying a desire to work with that scholar. For purposes of identifying individuals with military interests working in academia and for connecting scholars with places, the American Historical Association's *Guide to History Departments* is invaluable. Also useful is the online directory of the Society for Military History.[7]

Journals, Presses, and Associations

Academics and others interested in military history organize themselves not just in universities but also into specialist societies that promote and support their areas. It is often such societies that sponsor conferences and the publication of current research. This section surveys the most prominent of these organizations and the publishers that specialize in military history.

The flagship organization for military historians is the Society for Military History (SMH). As the Society's own publicity says:

> Established in 1933 as the American Military History Foundation, renamed in 1939 the American Military Institute, and renamed again in 1990 the Society for Military History, the Society is devoted to stimulating and advancing the study of military history. Its membership (today more than 2,300) has included many of the nation's most prominent scholars, soldiers, and citizens interested in military history.[8]

The SMH holds an annual conference and publishes the *Journal of Military History*. Although the conference programs and the contents of the *JMH* reflect the numerical preponderance of nineteenth- and twentieth-century historians in the membership of the society and among historians generally, the Society does include members from all chronological and geographic subfields of the discipline, and attempts, especially in its comprehensive book review section of the *JMH*, to cover all aspects of military history. Their website also maintains an extensive list of links to sources and research resources for military historians as well as links to other journals and societies in the field.

Given the chronological preponderance of modernists, however, it is not surprising that two of the most significant societies serving narrower groups of military historians are the Society of Ancient Military Historians (SAMH) and De Re

Militari: The Society for Medieval Military History, known among its members simply as De Re. The latter publishes an annual scholarly journal, *The Journal of Medieval Military History*. Both societies maintain websites[9] with links to resources tailored to their special interests; the De Re site has a very extensive and valuable online collection of both primary sources in translation and secondary articles and chapters of books. Both societies sponsor sessions at larger conferences: De Re sessions are a regular part of the program of the yearly International Medieval Congress in Kalamazoo, Michigan. For more recent military history there is the Company of Military Historians, a group of both collectors and military historians dedicated to studying the military material culture of the Americas,[10] and in Britain the Society for Army Historical Research, which focuses on the history of the British army and the armed forces of the Empire and Commonwealth.[11]

Partly because of the popular market, military history publishing is extensive. In terms of academic publishing, several scholarly journals, in addition to the ones mentioned above, are prominent among those serving the field. *War in History*, published by Arnold Publishers, covers the entire scope of the field just as the *JMH* does (though with something of the same modernist preponderance of articles). *Military History Quarterly* is aimed at a popular as well as a scholarly audience. And the US armed forces publish several scholarly journals aimed at professionals as well as academics, including *The Naval War College Review*, *Military Review*, the professional journal of the US army, prepared by US Army Command and General Staff College, and the air force's *Aerospace Power Journal*. Also well respected are the *Naval Institute Proceedings* and *Air University Review*. The *Air University Library Index to Military Periodicals*[12] has a useful though not exhaustive guide to many publications, with an emphasis on modern warfare.

Many publishers put out books in the field of military history, though only a few specialize in maintaining extensive lists in military history. Some sense of the major publishers in military history can be had through careful perusal of the notes and suggested readings in this book. Of particular note, Routledge puts out an impressive and high-quality series, called *Warfare and History*, edited by Jeremy Black, whose titles range all over the geographic and chronological maps of military history, reflecting Black's emphasis on global perspectives and his interest in warfare in all ages. In addition, Greenwood Publishing Group is a major publisher in military history, as is Westview Press. Boydell and Brewer, specialists in medieval history, have put out numerous books on medieval military history. Several university presses in the southern US publish regularly in American Civil War history, including Louisiana State University Press, University of Georgia Press, and University of North Carolina Press; others range more widely: Kansas, Nebraska, and Oklahoma all publish major series in military history, as does Cornell. Cambridge and Oxford, though hardly specializing in military history, nevertheless publish many important books in the field.

Students interested in doing military history face obstacles in academia, it is true. They also have opportunities and many points of entry and ways of obtaining more information, however. This chapter can provide no more than an introductory guide to those pathways, which are in any case constantly changing and expanding with the growth of academic military history generally. The key is to explore – with awareness of the general issues and contours of the field provided by this book – and let your enthusiasm guide you.

6

The Future of Military History

Predicting the future is not the job of historians, nor have they tended to be any better at it than anyone else. Understanding the past can enrich our understanding of how we got to where we are today, and even provides some general principles about historical development that can be used to think about the possible paths the human community might take in the future. But such principles are broad enough, and the number of possible future paths numerous enough, that no detailed prediction based on current conditions can ever hope to have more than general accuracy, and is likely to be significantly wrong. As for meteorologists, short-term forecasting, more highly constrained by current conditions, is somewhat easier and correspondingly more accurate. But long-range forecasts, either about the weather or about history, rapidly break down into little more than educated guesses. As chaotic systems (in the technical sense of chaos theory), both the weather and history resist detailed futurology.

So why write a chapter about the future of military history? In part, because the demands on the historical profession for guidance about future policy – and in international relations warfare and its future loom large in such considerations – are a known quantity, and we can thus sketch some of the potential directions in which military history will be drawn simply by assessing the current state of the world, sticking to a fairly short-term view. Some of these directions will by now, if this book has done its job, seem like logical extensions of what's going on in military history today. In part, however, discussion of the future of an academic field is less about scientific forecasting and more about normative agenda setting. In other words, when academics write about the current and future state of a field, what they really mean to do is say where the field *should* be going, rather than where it really might be going. And where an academic thinks the field should be going often proves to be a self-fulfilling prophecy about the future research and publishing plans of the predictor. So the reader is warned: herewith an inextricably interwoven combination of scientific historiographical prediction combined with a healthy dose of cheerleading.

Trends in the Field

We have already considered some of the current trends in military history in chapter 3. This academic context is one of the forces that will continue to exert pressure on military history in certain directions. Foremost on this list is the rising influence of cultural history, with its theoretical approaches to historical investigation, on future research in military history. For one thing, cultural history provides the natural entry point for gender studies to shape military history. The history of warrior elites in traditional societies, not to mention the public images of soldiers even in traditional and modern states without strong warrior elites, is intimately tied up with social constructions of masculinity. Research into the intersection of warfare, military cultures, and gender should prove to be a productive area for research. But the increasing role of women in modern armed forces also promises to broaden the discussion of gender and warfare to include women as fighters and the cultural implications of this very modern trend. Meanwhile, sadly, traditional intersections of warfare and gender, represented for example by the emergence of evidence of widespread rape and violence against women in the 1990s wars in Bosnia, may gain new prominence in this upsurge of war and gender studies.

Reinforcing the cultural turn is the charged cultural atmosphere of the so-called "Global War on Terror" that has followed the terrorist attacks of 9/11 and the ongoing war in Iraq. Although President George W. Bush quickly disavowed his use of the term "crusade" when he launched the war on terrorism, cultural attitudes linking warfare and religion are prominent in the current global climate and call for historicizing through careful studies of the longstanding connection between warfare and religious belief. More broadly, the apparent clash of cultures that many analysts see in the current Iraq insurgency and US attempts to pacify that country will continue to be part of the context that encourages studies of asymmetrical and unconventional warfare in which cultural attitudes form a crucial part of the problem.[1] The insights of postcolonial theory and cultural analysis more broadly will remain important tools for historians, not just in analyzing current conflicts but in reinterpreting colonial warfare and other historical instances of such conflicts. Given the organizational challenge militaries face in dealing with unconventional and asymmetrical warfare, it also seems likely that new approaches to institutional history will emerge as one way of understanding the possibilities for reorganizing systems of military force.

The "Global War on Terror" has implications not only for the increasing use of cultural analysis in military history, but also for the continued globalization of military history. Our survey of associations and publishers in chapter 5 was, the perceptive reader will have already noted, heavily Anglo-American. This is not just because of the English-language orientation of the authors, publisher, and audience of this book, but because Anglo-American and Western European military history remains more developed both as objects of study and as the geographic homes of academics who do military history. Both aspects of this dominance are changing already and are certain to continue changing. This will involve the development of a greater range of regional military histories, whether Asian, African, Latin American, or elsewhere, but will also advance by means of the new global perspectives being developed by world historians. And the number of perspectives and interpretations of military history will inevitably rise as scholars from around the world take up military history. This will allow more sophisticated and more solidly grounded comparative studies of the whole range of military history topics. Studies of military cultures, the relationship of armies and warrior elites to their societies, and of different forms of military organization, as well as the military meeting of different cultures, will undoubtedly benefit from this ongoing development.

In both of these trends, toward a greater impact of cultural history and toward greater globalization of military studies, there is a strong congruence between the theoretical interests and perspectives of academic historians on the one hand and the practical problems and interests of professional practitioners on the other. For both, the issues raised by terrorism, peacekeeping, nuclear proliferation, and nation-building will be prominent. The traditional core of military history, the study of battles and campaigns – broadly conceived so as to include cultural dimensions of how and why people fight (and why those people have traditionally been overwhelmingly male) – will likely remain vital. But the partial shift of interest away from the late 1990s concern with a revolution in military affairs toward terrorism-related and asymmetrical subjects, especially among writers closest to the practical end of military analysis, shows how much influence the current geopolitical climate can have on perceptions of what subjects within military history are most important to study. The longer-term trend that may be at work here, involving the decline of major wars between sophisticated technological equals (a trend that of course could rapidly and catastrophically reverse if things go badly wrong between, say, China and Taiwan), with such wars increasingly replaced by civil wars, guerilla fighting, and terrorist strikes, has potentially interesting implications for the traditional core of military history. Will the gradual disappearance of "traditional" wars (to take an optimistic view that may prove unfounded) make the traditional core of military history obsolete? Arguing against this possibility is the perceived necessity to remain prepared for such conflicts even if their occurrence seems unlikely, of course. And academic and popular interest in topics does not disappear with the decline of the phenomenon itself: histories of the African slave trade continue to be written, for example. Still, the question is interesting to consider, even if any answer necessarily is so long term as to be pure speculation.

In the shorter term, however, the congruence of academic and professional interest makes the forecasting of general trends relatively straightforward. Much more difficult is figuring out the trends in military history arising from the context of its popular audience and the media through which they are reached. What will the ongoing impact be of the History Channel (if any), for instance, or of the rising popularity of computer video games with military content? While fostering the longstanding popularity of military history among non-specialist audiences, it is not clear whether these new media will have any substantial impact on the way military history is practiced. One possibility, running somewhat counter to the trends emerging from academia and professional military history, is increasing emphasis on battles, tactics, and the technological face of military equipment. On the other hand, the continuing popularity of military history publications may reinforce the cross-fertilization of military history with social and cultural history. The historiography of the US Civil War provides a clue here: some of the richest and most popular works in that field – popular both with academic and general audiences – have been produced by academics who started in social history but moved to operational histories and military biographies to tap the popular market, and the Pulitzer Prize recently went to a military history of the American Revolution by a cultural historian.[2] Finally, the impact of the world wide web seems almost certain to be significant for professional practitioners, if only in making access to archival material steadily easier and more "democratic," as material is digitized and posted to websites.

The Politics of Military History

Ironically, perhaps, the democratization of access to military history archival material may contribute to the field's image problems within academia. For a field whose non-academic popularity already raises the specter of a lack of professionalism among academics, web archives might be seen as yet another manifestation of this problem. On the other hand, the fact that web-based sources are available for any field of history will mitigate this effect somewhat. But other aspects of the trends outlined above will also contribute to political questions for military history.

The major problem is the close association of academic and professional military historians in fact and perception, an association that casts the suspicion of collaboration with the "military industrial complex and the militarists in power" on those academics who do military history. In an academic world whose professorial politics are somewhat more liberal than those of the country at large, this can be a difficult perception for military historians to deal with, whatever their personal politics. Some, of course, will happily admit to such an intent and defend it. And indeed, there is a long history of academic studies of warfare influencing policy. Perhaps the most prominent case is the US naval build-up of the late nineteenth century, which gained significant interest from Alfred Thayer Mahan's studies of the influence of sea power on history and his numerous articles in popular magazines promoting American "navalism." (That this build-up quickly eventuated in one of the US's most imperialist wars also lends credence to the suspicions of antiwar academics.) Military history is certainly politically *relevant.*

But for exactly this reason, military history cannot afford to accept the perception that it is part of the "establishment." Nor should academic liberals dismiss it, for then they abandon a politically relevant field to their ideological opponents. As we asserted at the very beginning of this book, military historians come in all political persuasions, and their work ranges all over the map in its attitude toward current warfare. The migration of social and cultural historians to military history mentioned above simply adds to this diversity. Nobody, it is safe to say, celebrates warfare today in the way that warrior epics did in past cultures: the stakes and costs of modern war are too high for this to be a rational position. (It is possible to read, in their stress on the low human costs of an electronic battlefield, some of the enthusiasm for RMA ideas as a response to the costs of war argument at least for the technologically preponderant side, but this still falls somewhat short of outright celebration of war, and in fact implicitly concedes, if selfishly, the moral position that military deaths are a bad thing.) But some remain neutral, or at least do not express themselves, on the relevance of their studies of past warfare to the present, especially if they study ancient or medieval warfare. Many see war as a continuing necessary evil; among those, there is wide disagreement as to what level of threat constitutes necessity. Many are committed to peaceful foreign policy options in the present even as — in fact because — they study past wars. John Keegan's thoughtful piece on the increasing impossibility of human survival on the modern battlefield (and the question of the survival of the species in the event of a full-scale nuclear exchange between the 1976 superpowers) is a prominent example of military history as antiwar writing. Finally, many see war as an important part of human history and worthy of study just for that reason, which brings us back to the basic creative tension in the study of all history, including military history. We study the past to understand it on its own terms, and we study the past to learn about ourselves in the present. Military history is an important and necessary part of that study from both perspectives, and will continue to be so. That's the present and the future of military history.

Notes

Chapter 2 Military Historiography

1 Herodotus, *The Histories*, trans. Aubrey de Selencourt (Penguin, 1954), 41.

2 Thucydides, *History of the Peloponnesian War*, trans. Rex Warner (Penguin, 1954), 35.

3 Ibid., 47.

4 Ibid., 392–3 (Bk V c. 71).

5 See Xenophon, *Anabasis*, ed. and trans. Carleton Brownson; rev. edn. by John Dillery (Loeb Classical Library: Harvard University Press, 1998) and *The Art of Horsemanship*, trans. M. H. Morgan (Sidney Smith, 1999).

6 Caesar, *The Gallic Wars*, trans. Carolyn Hammond (Oxford University Press, 1996).

7 Caesar, *The Civil War*, trans. Jane F. Mitchell (Penguin, 1967).

8 E.g. Plutarch, *Plutarch's Lives*, ed. Arthur Clough, trans. John Dryden, 2 vols (Modern Library, 2001).

9 Among many editions and selections by each author, see, for example: Sallust, *Sallust*, trans. J. C. Rolfe (Loeb 116: Harvard University Press, 1921); Livy, *The Early History of Rome*, trans. Aubrey de Selincourt (Penguin, 2002) and *The War with Hannibal*, trans. Aubrey de Selincourt (Penguin, 1965); Tacitus, *The Annals of Imperial Rome*, trans. Michael Grant (Penguin, 1956); Josephus, *The Works of Josephus*, trans. William Whiston (Hendrickson Publishers, 1980); Ammianus Marcellinus, *The Later Roman Empire: AD 354–378*, trans. Walter Hamilton (Penguin, 1986).

10 Flavius Renatus Vegetius, *Epitome of Military Science*, trans. N. P. Milner (Liverpool University Press, 1993).

11 Sun-Tzu, *The Art of War*, trans. Roger Ames (Classics of Ancient China: Ballantine, 1993).

12 Sima Qian, *Records of the Grand Historian*, trans. Burton Watson (Columbia University Press, 1993).

13 A few of the better histories from this period are Gregory of Tours, *A History of the Franks*, trans. Lewis Thorpe (Penguin, 1976); Flodoard of Reims, *The Annals of Flodoard of Reims, 191–966*, trans. Bernard Bachrach and Steven Fanning (Broadview Press, 2004); *The Anglo-Saxon Chronicle*, trans. Michael Swanton (Routledge, 1998).

14 *The Song of Roland*, trans. Glyn Burgess (Penguin, 1990). *Roland* is biased toward a strong king; for a more aristocratic perspective (and less skillful poetry), compare *Raoul de Cambrai*, trans. Sarah Key (Oxford University Press, 1992). See also the more literary Anglo-Saxon tradition represented by *The Battle of Maldon*, trans. Bill Griffiths (Harry Ransom Humanities Research Center: December, 2000).

15 *Sundiata: An Epic of Old Mali*, trans. D. T. Niane (Longman, 1995); and, e.g., *The Tale of the Heike*, trans. Helen McCullough (Stanford University Press, 1988).

16 William of Poitiers, *The Gesta Guillelmi of William of Poitiers*, trans. R. H. C. Davis and Marjorie Chibnall (Oxford Medieval Texts, 1998); Orderic Vitalis, *The Ecclesiastical History*, trans. Marjorie Chibnall, 6 vols. (Oxford University Press, 1969–80); William of Malmesbury, *Gesta regum Anglorum*, ed. and trans. R. A. B. Mynors, R. M. Thomson, and M. Winterbottom (Oxford, 1998); among Crusade historians, see Fulcher of Chartres, *The First Crusade: The Chronicle of Fulcher of Chartres*, trans. Edward Peters, 2nd edn. (University of Pennsylvania Press, 1998).

17 Jean Froissart, *Chronicles*, trans. Geoffrey Brereton (Penguin, 1978).

18 Procopius, *The Secret History*, trans. G. A. Williamson (Penguin, 1982); Michael Psellus, *Fourteen Byzantine Rulers: The Chronographia of Michael Psellus*, trans. E. R. A. Sewter (Penguin, 1979); Anna Comnena, *The Alexiad*, trans. E. R. A. Sewter (Penguin, 1979).

19 See for example *Maurice's Strategikon: Handbook of Byzantine Military Strategy*, trans. George Dennis (University of Pennsylvania Press, 2001) and *Sowing the Dragon's Teeth: Byzantine Warfare in the Tenth Century*, trans. Eric McGeer (Geneological Publishing Company, 1995).

20 See for example *Digeneis Akritas: The Two-Blood Border Lord*, trans. Denison Hull (Ohio University Press, 1986).

21 Ibn al-Athir, *The Annals of the Saljuq Turks: Selections from al-Kamil fi'l Fa'rikh of Ibn al-Athir*, trans. D. S. Richards (Curzon Press, 2002).

22 Ibn Khaldun, *The Muqaddima*, trans. Franz Rosenthal (Bollingen, 1969).

23 Machiavelli, *The Prince*, trans. Daniel Donno (Bantam, 1984); *The Art of War*, trans. Ellis Farneworth (Da Capo Press, 2001); *Discourses on Livy*, trans. Harvey Mansfield (University of Chicago Press, 1998).

24 Available in modern edition as David Hume, *The History of England, from the Invasion of Julius Caesar to the Revolution in 1688* (Liberty Classics, 1983).

25 Available in abridged form: Edward Gibbon, *History of the Decline and Fall of the Roman Empire* (Penguin, 2001).

26 For Montecuccoli and his contributions, see Azar Gat, *The Origins of Military Thought from the Enlightenment to Clausewitz* (Oxford, 1989), 13–24, and Gunther E. Rothenberg, "Maurice of Nassau, Gustavus Adolphus, Raimondo Montecuccoli, and the 'Military Revolution' of the Seventeenth Century," in Peter Paret, ed., *The Makers of Modern Strategy from Machiavelli to the Nuclear Age* (Princeton, 1986), 32–63, esp. 59–63.

27 For the numbers of works published and an excellent overview of the key individuals and their writings, see Gat, *Origins of Military Thought*, 25–94.

28 Baron Antoine Henri Jomini, *The Art of War* (Greenhill Press, 1971); Carl von Clausewitz, *On War*, ed. and trans. Michael Howard and Peter Paret (Princeton, 1976).

29 Alfred Thayer Mahan, *The Influence of Sea Power Upon History, 1660–1783* (Dover Publications, 1987); Sir Julian Corbett, *Principles of Maritime Strategy* (Dover Publications, 2004).

30 Available in modern translation as Hans Delbrück, *History of the Art of War*, trans. Walter Renfroe, 3 vols. (University of Nebraska Press, 1990–7).

31 The following discussion is based on John Keegan, *The Face of Battle* (Penguin, 1976), 55–8; the entire introductory chapter of this book is an important historiographical analysis of military history up to the time of the book's publication; see p. 41 below.

32 Sir Edward Creasy, *Fifteen Decisive Battles of the World: From Marathon to Waterloo*, reprint edn. (Da Capo Press, 1994).

33 Probably the best known and most successful is Major General

J. F. C. Fuller, *A Military History of the Western World*, 3 vols (Eyre & Spottiswoode, 1954–6).

34 Not only are Creasy and Fuller still available in modern reprint editions and receiving favorable reviews from readers on the Amazon.com website, but new works in the genre continue to appear: see, for example, the popular magazine *Military History*, which regularly publishes special "Great Battles" issues.

35 It, too, is still readily available: Sir Charles Oman, *A History of the Art of War in the Middle Ages: 378–1278* AD (Greenhill Books, 1999).

36 Stephen Morillo, *The Battle of Hastings: Source and Interpretations* (Boydell and Brewer, 1996), 149–64, on the debate between Charles Freeman and J. H. Round and a selection from Freeman's narrative of the battle itself.

37 Bell I. Wiley, *The Life of Johnny Reb: The Common Soldier of the Confederacy* (Louisiana State University Press, reissue edn., 1979; first published in 1943); *The Life of Billy Yank: The Common Soldier of the Union* (Louisiana State University Press, reissue edn., 1979; first published in 1952).

38 Some of the prominent names include B. H. Liddell Hart, Cyril Falls, Theodore Ropp, Walter Millis, and Bernard Brodie; see Suggestions for Further Readings for more references.

39 H. J. Hewitt, *The Organization of War under Edward III* (Manchester University Press, 1958); Warren Hollister, *Anglo-Saxon Military Institutions on the Eve of the Norman Conquest* (Oxford University Press, 1962) and *The Military Organization of Norman England* (Oxford University Press, 1964); R. C. Smail, *Crusading Warfare, 1097–1193* (Cambridge University Press, 1959).

40 See note 31 above.

41 Geoffrey Parker, *The Military Revolution. Military Innovation and the Rise of the West, 1500–1800* (Cambridge University Press, 1988).

42 Michael Roberts, "The Military Revolution, 1560–1660," in *Essays in Swedish History* (University of Minnesota Press, 1967), 195–225, a revision of an inaugural lecture delivered at The Queen's University, Belfast in January, 1955. Similar themes were explored a decade after Roberts from the global perspective that Parker adopted, by Carlo Cipolla, *Guns, Sails and Empires: Technological Innovation and the Early Phases of European Expansion, 1400–1700* (Minerva Press, 1967).

Chapter 3   Conceptual Frameworks

1   For a discussion and critique of the concept of "decisiveness" as applied to battles, see Stephen Morillo, ed., *The Battle of Hastings: Sources and Interpretations* (Boydell and Brewer, 1996), xv–xvii. And see, for example, Barry Strauss, *The Battle of Salamis. The Naval Encounter that Saved Greece – and Western Civilization* (Simon and Schuster, 2004), 247. Strauss in fact claims that a Greek loss at Salamis and Persian conquest of the Peloponnese would have had little effect on the long-term development of Greek civilization or the course of history. Particular wars and war more generally have certainly been important influences on the course of history, but individual battles – even "great" ones – are generally overrated.

2   An impact summed up by the title of Bernard Brodie's *From Crossbow to H-bomb* (Indiana University Press, 1973), a study of military technology through the ages.

3   A very good discussion of the questions summarized in the following paragraphs can be found in Guy Halsall, *Warfare and Society in the Barbarian West, 450–900* (Warfare and History: Routledge, 2003).

4   An issue explored further in Stephen Morillo, "Contrary Winds: Theories of History and the Limits of *Sachkritik*," in M. Ragnow, ed., *Essays in Honor of Bernard Bachrach* (forthcoming), and N. Whatley, "On the Possibility of Reconstructing Marathon and Other Ancient Battles," *The Journal of Hellenic Studies* 84 (1964), 119–39.

5   See the discussion in Stephen Morillo, "Milites, Knights and Samurai: Military Terminology, Comparative History, and the Problem of Translation," in B. Bachrach and R. Abels, eds, *The Normans and their Adversaries at War: Essays in Honor of C. Warren Hollister* (Boydell and Brewer, 2001), 167–84.

6   An interesting explication of Roman grand strategy, one which has aroused much argument among specialists in Roman history as to whether such a thing in fact existed, is outlined in Edward N. Luttwak, *The Grand Strategy of the Roman Empire from the First Century to the Third* (Johns Hopkins University Press, 1976). Luttwak's analytical toolkit has been applied with equally interesting results in John P. Le Donne, *The Grand Strategy of the Russian Empire, 1650–1831* (Oxford University Press, 2004). Le Donne meets some of the objections raised by classicists about the Roman case – that the Romans formulated no explicit grand strategy and that the patterns Luttwak cites in support of

his case emerged from local, ad hoc decisions based in cultural rather than strategic principles – by arguing that a grand strategy need not be fully conscious to be nevertheless extant, coherent and analyzable. For a defense of Roman grand strategy, also worth considering are the excellent article by Everett L. Wheeler, "Methodological Limits and the Mirage of Roman Strategy," *The Journal of Military History* 57. 1 (1993), 7–41 and 57. 2 (1993), 215–40, and the overview by Michael Pavkovic, "Roman Grand Strategy," *Military Chronicles* 1. 1 (2005), 14–30.

7   Clifford Rogers, "The Bergerac Campaign and Henry of Lancaster," *Journal of Medieval Military History* 2 (2004), 89–110 at 97.

8   The foundational studies of logistics are Donald Engels, *Alexander the Great and the Logistics of the Macedonian Army* (University of California Press, 1978) and Martin van Creveld, *Supplying War: Logistics from Wallenstein to Patton* (Cambridge University Press, 1979). See also John Haldon, *Warfare, State and Society in the Byzantine World, 565–1204* (Warfare and History: Routledge, 1999), 158–76, for some corrections to Engels's figures; and John Lynn, ed., *Feeding Mars: Logistics in Western Warfare from the Middle Ages to the Present* (Westview Press, 1994).

9   Concern about the mutual interests of arms suppliers and factions within the state dates at least to eighteenth-century England: see John Brewer, *The Sinews of Power. War, Money and the English State, 1688–1783* (Harvard University Press, 1988), ch. 8. The relationship of Halliburton to the second Bush administration and the second Iraq war are almost too obvious to need mentioning in this context.

10   John Lynn, *Battle: A History of Combat and Culture* (Perseus Books Group, 2003) provides a number of case studies drawn from throughout history.

11   The idea of the "military horizon" and the historiography associated with it is discussed in John Keegan, *A History of Warfare* (Knopf, 1993), ch. 1.

12   See Lawrence Keely, *War before Civilization: The Myth of the Peaceful Savage* (Oxford University Press, 1997) and Steven LeBlanc and Katherine Register, *Constant Battles: The Myth of the Peaceful, Noble Savage* (St Martin's, 2003) on one side, and Brian Ferguson and Neil Whitehead, eds, *War in the Tribal Zone: Expanding States and Indigenous Warfare* (School of American Research Press, 1992), as well as other articles by Ferguson, on the other; see also Jonathan Haas, *The Anthropology of War* (Cambridge University Press, 1990). The gap between the two

sides may not be as wide as the mutual polemics assert, as almost all of Keely's evidence, for example, can be fit into Ferguson's conceptual and chronological framework.

13 Bengt Thordeman and Brian R. Price, *Armour from the Battle of Wisby* (Chivalry Bookshelf, 2001).

14 The best archaeological studies of Little Big Horn are Douglas D. Scott, P. Willey, and Melissa A. Connor, *They Died with Custer. Soldiers' Bones from the Battle of the Little Bighorn* (University of Oklahoma Press, 1998); Gregory F. Michno, *Lakota Noon: The Indian Narrative of Custer's Defeat* (Mountain Press, 1997); and Douglas D. Scott, Richard A. Fox, Jr., Melissa A. Connor, and Dick Harmon, *Archaeological Perspectives on the Battle of the Little Bighorn* (University of Oklahoma Press, 1989). See also Richard Allan Fox, Jr., *Archaeology, History, and Custer's Last Battle: The Little Big Horn Reexamined* (University of Oklahoma Press, 1993).

15 See J. S. Morrison, J. F. Coates, and N. B. Rankov, *The Athenian Trireme: the History and Reconstruction of an Ancient Greek Warship* (Cambridge University Press, 2000).

16 See, for example, Geoffrey Blainey, *The Causes of War* (Free Press, 1988). The vast war and state formation literature often orbits around the work of Charles Tilly: see his *Coercion, Capital, and European States*, AD 990–1990 (Blackwell, 1990).

17 Michael Mann, *The Sources of Social Power* (Cambridge University Press, 1986) is an important sociological examination of power, both military and otherwise, in pre-industrial history, for example.

18 Michael P. Speidel, "Berserks: A History of Indo-European 'Mad Warriors'," *Journal of World History* 13 (2002), 253–91, and more fully developed in *Ancient Germanic Warriors: Warrior Styles from Trajan's Column to Icelandic Sagas* (Routledge, 2004); Jonathan Shay, *Achilles in Vietnam: Combat Trauma and the Undoing of Character* (Scribner, 1995).

19 See for example Richard Abels' use of regression analysis of Domesday Book (1085) evidence for land values and thus economic obligations for military service in his "Bookland and Fyrd Service in Late Saxon England," in Morillo, ed., *Battle of Hastings*, 57–78.

20 Alan Munslow, *Deconstructing History* (Routledge, 1997), is a valuable introduction to this topic, as is Peter Burke, *What is Cultural History?* (Polity Press, 2004).

21 Jeremy Black, *Rethinking Military History* (Routledge, 2004). For a new synthesis of global military history that addresses all of these issues, see Stephen Morillo, Michael F. Pavkovic, and

Paul Lococo, *War in World History: Society, Technology and War from Ancient Times to the Present* (McGraw-Hill, forthcoming).

22   Stephen Morillo, "Guns and Government: A Comparative Study of Europe and Japan," *Journal of World History* 6 (1995), 75–106, for a case study containing more specific discussion of such problems; and Morillo, "Milites, Knights and Samurai" on terminological problems.

23   Elizabeth A. R. Brown, "The Tyranny of a Construct: Feudalism and Historians of Medieval Europe," *American Historical Review* 70 (1955), 353–98; Susan Reynolds, *Fiefs and Vassals: The Medieval Evidence Reinterpreted* (Oxford University Press, 1996); Stephen Morillo, "A 'Feudal Mutation'? Conceptual Tools and Historical Patterns in World History," *Journal of World History* 14 (2003), 531–50.

24   Some recent major works of global and comparative military history include Jeremy Black, *War and the World. Military Power and the Fate of Continents, 1450–2000* (Yale University Press, 1998); David Ralston, *Importing the European Army: The Introduction of European Military Techniques and Institutions in the Extra-European World, 1600–1914* (University of Chicago Press, 1996); and Christon I. Archer, John R. Ferris, et al., *World History of Warfare* (University of Nebraska Press, 2002). The last is ambitious but flawed by Eurocentrism and a quirky focus. A more truly global and comparative global history of warfare is Morillo, Pavkovic, and Lococo, *War in World History*.

25   Morillo, "Guns and Government"; cf. Kenneth Chase, *Firearms. A Global History to 1700* (Cambridge University Press, 2003).

Chapter 4   Current Controversies

1   Kelly DeVries, "Catapults Are Not Atomic Bombs: Towards a Redefinition of 'Effectiveness' in Premodern Military Technology," *War in History* 4 (1997), 454–70; Clifford Rogers, "The Efficacy of the English Longbow: A Reply to Kelly DeVries," *War in History* 5 (1998), 233–42.

2   Terence Zuber, *Inventing the Schlieffen Plan: German War Planning, 1871–1914* (Oxford University Press, 2003); Terence Holmes, "The Real Thing: A Reply to Terence Zuber's 'Terence Holmes Reinvents the Schlieffen Plan'," *War in History* 9 (2002), 111–20, and a series of further articles in *War in History*.

3   Much of the relevant literature, including Roberts's seminal article, are collected in Clifford Rogers, ed., *The Military*

Revolution Debate (Westview Press, 1995).

4   Geoffrey Parker, "The 'Military Revolution, 1560–1660' – A Myth?," reprinted in Rogers, ed., *Military Revolution Debate.*

5   William McNeill, *The Pursuit of Power: Technology, Armed Force, and Society since AD 1000* (University of Chicago Press, 1984).

6   Jeremy Black, "A Military Revolution? A 1660–1792 Perspective," in Rogers, ed., *Military Revolution Debate*; see also Black, *A Military Revolution? Military Change and European Society, 1550–1800* (Palgrave Macmillan, 1991), among many other books where Black deals with the topic.

7   For a useful overview, see Williamson Murray and MacGregor Knox, eds., *The Dynamics of Military Revolution, 1300–2050* (Cambridge University Press, 2001).

8   Clifford Rogers, "The Military Revolutions of the Hundred Years War," in Rogers, ed., *Military Revolution Debate*; cf. Murray and Knox, *Dynamics of Military Revolution.*

9   Kenneth Chase, *Firearms. A Global History to 1700* (Cambridge University Press, 2003).

10 See for example Robert Drews, *The End of the Bronze Age* (Princeton University Press, 1995).

11 The RMA debate has its own website: <http://www.comw.org /rma/>, with numerous links to articles and resources. A good early review of the debate that contextualizes it against other "military revolution" literature is Eliot Cohen, "A Revolution in Warfare," *Foreign Affairs* 75 (1996), 37–54.

12 But see Ahmed S. Hashim, "The Revolution in Military Affairs Outside the West," *Journal of International Affairs* 51 (1998), 431–45.

13 Stephen Budiansky, *Air Power* (Viking, 2004) summarizes very well the history and historiography of air power and its proponents. See also John Buckley, *Air Power in the Age of Total War, 1900–60* (War and History: Routledge, 1999).

14 See most recently Frederick Taylor, *Dresden, Tuesday, February 13, 1945* (HarperCollins, 2004).

15 Seminally, Lynn White, *Medieval Technology and Social Change* (Oxford University Press, 1962). A key refutation is Bernard Bachrach, "Charles Martel, Shock Combat, the Stirrup, and Feudalism," *Studies in Medieval and Renaissance History* 7 (1970), 47–75.

16 Daniel Dennett, *Darwin's Dangerous Idea: Evolution and the Meanings of Life* (Simon and Schuster, 1996).

17 John Thornton, "The Art of War in Angola," *Comparative Studies in Society and History* 30 (1988), 360–78; Stephen

Morillo, "Guns and Government: A Comparative Study of Europe and Japan," *Journal of World History* 6 (1995), 75–106.

18 Victor Davis Hanson, *The Western Way of War. Infantry Battle in Classical Greece* (Knopf, 1989). Hanson was trained as a philologist.

19 See most recently and forcefully Hans van Wees, *Greek Warfare. Myths and Realities* (Duckworth, 2004).

20 Hanson, *Why the West Has Won: Nine Landmark Battles in the Brutal History of Western Victory* (Faber and Faber, 2002); *Carnage and Culture: Landmark Battles in the Rise of Western Power* (Anchor, 2002).

21 John Lynn, *Battle: A History of Combat and Culture* (Perseus Books Group, 2003).

22 Geoffrey Parker, ed., *The Cambridge Illustrated History of Warfare* (Cambridge University Press, 2000).

23 Edward Said, *Orientalism* (Vintage, 1979).

24 Robert Citino, *Blitzkrieg to Desert Storm. The Evolution of Operational Warfare* (University Press of Kansas, 2004) is particularly good on this issue.

25 Lynn, *Battle*, ch. 6; cf. Dirk H. A. Kolff, *Naukar, Rajput, and Sepoy: The Ethnohistory of the Military Labour Market of Hindustan, 1450–1850* (Cambridge University Press, 2002).

26 Thomas P. M. Barnett, *The Pentagon's New Map* (Putnam, 2004).

27 Lynn, *Battle*, Appendix.

28 See Bernard Bachrach, *Early Medieval Warfare: Prelude to Empire* (University of Pennsylvania Press, 2001); Charles R. Bowlus, *Franks, Moravians and Magyars. The Struggle for the Middle Danube 788–907* (University of Pennsylvania Press, 1995); K. F. Werner, "Heersorganisation und Kriegsführung im deutschen Königsreich de 10. und 11. Jahrhunderts," *Settimane di Studio del Centro Italiano di Studi sull'Alto Medioevo* 15 (Spoleto, 1968).

29 See above all Guy Halsall, *Warfare and Society in the Barbarian West, 450–900* (Warfare and History: Routledge, 2003), and literature he cites; see also Richard Abels, *Lordship and Military Obligation in Anglo-Saxon England* (University of California Press, 1988).

30 Richard Abels and Stephen Morillo, "A Lying Legacy: Images of Antiquity and Altered Reality in Medieval Military History," *Journal of Medieval Military History* 3 (2005), 1–18.

31 See John France, "Recent Writing on Medieval Warfare: From the Fall of Rome to c.1300," *Journal of Military History* 65 (2001), 441–73.

32 John Haldon, *Warfare, State and Society in the Byzantine World, 565–1204* (Warfare and History: Routledge, 1999); Mark Whittow, *The Making of Orthodox Byzantium, 600–1025* (University of California Press, 1996) Hugh Kennedy, *The Armies of the Caliphs* (War and History: Routledge, 2001); cf. Warren Treadgold, *Byzantium and Its Army 284–1081* (Stanford University Press, 1999).

33 See n. 15 above.

34 Noel Perrin, *Giving Up the Gun: Japan's Reversion to the Sword, 1543–1879* (David R. Godine Publisher, 1995).

35 Morillo, "Guns and Government"; in somewhat different form, Chase, *Firearms.*

36 This constellation could also include the related but essentially non-military topic of the Holocaust.

37 Citino, *Blitzkrieg to Desert Storm.*

38 Barry Posen, *The Sources of Military Doctrine: France, Britain and Germany between the World Wars* (Cornell University Press, 1984); cf. Stephen Rosen, *Winning the Next War: Innovation and the Modern Military* (Cornell University Press, 1991).

39 Larry Addington, *The Blitzkrieg Era and the German General Staff, 1865–1941* (Rutgers University Press, 1971).

40 James Corum, *The Roots of Blitzkrieg: Hans von Seeckt and German Military Reform* (University Press of Kansas, 1992).

41 Albert Seaton and Joan Seaton, *The Soviet Army. 1918 to the Present* (New American Library, 1986).

42 Mary R. Habeck, *Storm of Steel. The Development of Armor Doctrine in Germany and the Soviet Union, 1919–1939* (Cornell University Press, 2003).

43 John Mosier, *The Blitzkrieg Myth. How Hitler and the Allies Misread the Strategic Realities of World War II* (HarperCollins, 2003).

44 Alexander B. Rossino, *Hitler Strikes Poland. Blitzkrieg, Ideology, Atrocity* (University Press of Kansas, 2003).

45 Citino, *Blitzkrieg to Desert Storm.*

46 Geoffrey Wawro, *The Franco-Prussian War: The German Conquest of France in 1870–1871* (Cambridge University Press, 2003); Michael Howard, *Franco-Prussian War: The German Invasion of France 1870–1871,* rev. edn. (Routledge, 2001).

47 Niall Ferguson, *The Pity of War: Explaining World War I* (Basic Books, 2000).

Chapter 5   Doing Military History

1   John France, *Western Warfare in the Age of the Crusades, 1000–1300* (Cornell University Press, 1999).

2   Victor Davis Hanson, *A War Like no Other: How the Athenians and Spartans Fought the Peloponnesian War* (Random House, 2005).

3   The Bayeux Tapestry on CD-Rom (Scholarly Digital Editions, 2002).

4   Stephen Morillo, "Milites, Knights and Samurai: Military Terminology, Comparative History, and the Problem of Translation," in B. Bachrach and R. Abels, eds, *The Normans and their Adversaries at War: Essays in Honor of C. Warren Hollister* (Boydell and Brewer, 2001), 167–84.

5   Robin Higham, *Official Military Historical Offices and Sources*: Volume I: *Europe, Africa, the Middle East, and India* (Greenwood Press, 2000) and *Official Military Historical Offices and Sources*: Volume II: *The Western Hemisphere and the Pacific Rim* (Greenwood Press, 2000) are excellent guides to the official archives of military history sources. The same author's *A Guide to the Sources of United States Military History* (Shoe String Press, 1976) and *A Guide to the Sources of British Military History* (University of California Press, 1972), each now with several updated supplements, cover an even broader range of sources.

6   The Society for Military History online guide can be found at: <http://www.smh-hq.org/gradguide/index.html>. Their listing of graduate programs included, as of August 2005, the following: Bilkent University, Brigham Young University, Canadian Forces College, Duke University, East Tennessee State University, George Washington University, Hawaii Pacific University, Kansas State University, King's College London, The Ohio State University, Ohio University, Penn State University, Royal Military College of Canada, Sam Houston State University, Scottish Centre for War Studies, Temple University, Texas A&M University, Texas Christian University, Texas Tech University, University of Houston, University of Indianapolis, University of Kansas, University of Nebraska-Lincoln, University of New Mexico, University of North Carolina-Chapel Hill, University of North Texas, University of Salford, University of South Alabama, University of South Dakota, University of Southern Mississippi, University of Tennessee.

7   The Society for Military History online directory can be found

at: <http://www.smh-hq.org/directory/index.html>.
8 <http://www.smh-hq.org/index.html>.
9 SAMH: <http://ccat.sas.upenn.edu/rrice/samh.html>. De Re: <http://www.deremilitari.org/>; Stephen Morillo is President of De Re.
10 Company of Military Historians: <http://military-historians. org/>.
11 Society for Armed Historical Research: <http://www.sahr.co. uk/>.
12 *Air University Library Index to Military Periodicals*: <http://www.dtic.mil/dtic/aulimp/>.

Chapter 6 The Future of Military History

1 See for example, Roger Barnett, *Asymmetical Warfare: Today's Challenge to US Military Power* (Brassey's Inc., 2003).
2 Civil War historians who started in social history include James McPherson, whose *Battle Cry of Freedom: The Civil War Era* (Oxford University Press, 1988) won the Pulitzer; Emory Thomas, *Robert E. Lee: A Biography* (W. W. Norton, 1995), exemplifies the biographical approach. David Hackett Fischer, *Washington's Crossing* (Oxford University Press, 2004) is the more recent Pulitzer winner.

Suggestions for Further Reading

No list of suggestions for further reading can be comprehensive, and any selection will leave some perspective shorted or someone's classic, must-read book off the list. This list should therefore be read simply as what it claims to be: a list of suggestions that does not pretend to be definitive. Dividing such a list up into subsections is equally problematic, as many books will fit in a variety of categories, no matter what the system of classification. The system below seemed convenient, to us, for newcomers to the field.

Battles and Campaigns

Andradé, Dale. *America's Last Vietnam Battle: Halting Hanoi's 1972 Easter Offensive*. University Press of Kansas, 2001.

Asprey, R. *At Belleau Wood*. University of North Texas Press, 1996.

Bowlus, C.R. *Franks, Moravians and Magyars. The Struggle for the Middle Danube 788–907*. University of Pennsylvania Press, 1995.

Chandler, D. *The Campaigns of Napoleon*. Weidenfeld and Nicolson, 1966.

Coddington, E. *The Gettysburg Campaign: A Study in Command*. Touchstone, 1996.

Corbett, J. *The Campaign of Trafalgar*. Trafalgar Square Publishing, 2005.

Daly, G. *Cannae: the Experience of Battle in the Second Punic War*. Routledge, 2002.

D'Este, C. *Decision in Normandy*. Perennial, 1984.

Doherty, R. *The Williamite War in Ireland 1688–1691*. Four Courts Press, 1998.

France, J. *Victory in the East: a Military History of the First Crusade*. Cambridge University Press, 1996.

Gallagher, Gary W. *Chancellorsville: The Battle and its Aftermath*. University of North Carolina Press, 1996.

Gallagher, Gary W., ed. *The Antietam Campaign*. University of North Carolina Press, 1999.

Gill, J. *With Eagles to Glory*. Greenhill Books, 1992.

Glantz, D. M. *The Initial Period of the War on the Eastern Front: 22 June–August, 1941*. Frank Cass Publishers, 1993.

Hammond, N. G. L. *The Genius of Alexander the Great*. University of North Carolina Press, 1997.

Hanson, V. D. *A War Like No Other: How the Athenians and Spartans Fought the Peloponnesian War*. Random House, 2005.

Keegan, J. *The Face of Battle*. Penguin, 1976.

Lambert, A. *Dreadnought Gunnery and the Battle of Jutland: the Question of Fire Control*. Routledge, 2005.

Leggiere, Michael V. *Napoleon and Berlin: The Franco-Prussian War in North Germany, 1813*. University of Oklahoma Press, 2002.

Lehrack, O. *No Shining Armor. The Marines in Vietnam: An Oral History*. University Press of Kansas, 1992.

Lendon, E. *Soldiers and Ghosts: A History of Battle in Classical Antiquity*. Yale University Press, 2005.

Lewis, A. *Omaha Beach: A Flawed Victory*. University of North Carolina Press, 2001.

Linderman, G. *The World within War: America's Combat Experience in World War II*. Free Press, 1997.

Linn, B. *The Philippine War, 1899–1902*. University Press of Kansas, 2000.

Lloyd, A. B. *Battle in Antiquity*. Focus Publishing, 1997.

Morillo, Stephen, ed. *The Battle of Hastings: Sources and Interpretations*. Boydell and Brewer, 1996.

Muir, R. *Salamanca 1812*. Yale University Press, 2001.

Padfield, P. *Maritime Power and Struggle for Freedom: Naval Campaigns that Shaped the Modern World 1788–1851*. Overlook Hardcover, 2005.

Riley, J. P. *Napoleon and the World War of 1813: Lessons in Coalition Warfighting*. Frank Cass Publishers, 2000.

Schneid, F. *Napoleon's Italian campaigns: 1805–1815*. Praeger Publishers, 2002.

Schneid, F. *Napoleon's Conquest of Europe: The War of the Third Coalition*. Praeger Publishers, 2005.

Showalter, D. *Tannenberg. Clash of Empires.* Revised edn, Potomac Books, 2004.

Siborne, W. *History of the Waterloo Campaign.* Greenhill Books, 1995.

Sledge, E. B. *With the Old Breed: At Peleliu and Okinawa.* Oxford University Press, 1990.

Spector, R. *Eagle Against the Sun.* Vintage, 1985.

Strachan, H. *World War I.* Viking, 2003.

Strauss, B. *The Battle of Salamis. The Naval Encounter that Saved Greece – and Western Civilization.* Simon and Schuster, 2004.

Taylor, F. *Dresden, Tuesday, February 13, 1945.* HarperCollins, 2004.

Warner, D. and P. Warner, *The Tide at Sunrise: A History of the Russo-Japanese War, 1904–1905.* Frank Cass & Co, 2002, reprint.

Wawro, G. *Austro-Prussian War: Austria's War with Prussia and Italy in 1866.* Cambridge University Press, 1996.

Wawro, G. *The Franco-Prussian War: Germany Conquers France in 1870–71.* Cambridge University Press, 2003.

Webster, G. *The Roman Invasion of Britain.* Routledge, 1980.

Weigley, R. *The Age of Battles: The Quest for Decisive Warfare from Breitenfeld to Waterloo.* Indiana University Press, 1991.

Wells, P. *The Battle That Stopped Rome: Emperor Augustus, Arminius, and the Slaughter of the Legions in the Teutoburg Forest.* W. W. Norton & Company, 2003

Strategy and Tactics

Addington, L. *The Blitzkrieg Era and the German General Staff, 1865–1941.* Rutgers University Press, 1971.

Anderson, J. K. *Military Theory and Practice in the Age of Xenophon.* University of California Press, 1970.

Buckley, J. *Air Power in the Age of Total War, 1900–60.* Routledge, 1999.

Budiansky, S. *Air Power.* Viking, 2004.

Chandler, D. *The Art of War in the Age of Marlborough.* Sarpedon Publishers, 1976.

Citino, R. *Quest for Decisive Victory: from Stalemate to Blitzkrieg in Europe, 1899–1940.* University Press of Kansas, 2002.

Citino, R. *Blitzkrieg to Desert Storm. The Evolution of Operational Warfare.* University Press of Kansas, 2004.

Corum, J. *The Roots of Blitzkrieg: Hans von Seeckt and German Military Reform.* University Press of Kansas, 1992.

Crane, Conrad. *American Airpower Strategy in Korea, 1950–1953.* University Press of Kansas, 2000.

Ducrey, P. *Warfare in Ancient Greece.* Schocken, 1986.

Echevarria, Antulio J. *After Clausewitz: German Military Thinkers Before the Great War.* University Press of Kansas, 2000.

Gat, A. *The Origins of Military Thought.* Oxford University Press, 1989.

Gooch, John, ed. *Airpower: Theory and Practice.* Frank Cass Publishers, 1995.

Gray, C. *The Leverage of Sea Power.* Free Press, 1992.

Gray, C. *Weapons Don't Make War: Policy, Strategy, and Military Technology.* University Press of Kansas, 1993.

Griffith, P. *Battle Tactics of the Civil War.* Yale University Press, 1989.

Griffith, P. *Forward into Battle: Fighting Tactics from Waterloo to the Nuclear Age.* Presidio Press, 1991.

Guderian, H. *Achtung Panzer: The Development of Armored Forces. Their Tactics and Operational Potential.* Sterling 1995.

Gudmundsson, B. I. *Stormtroop Tactics: Innovation in the German Army, 1914–1918.* Praeger Paperback, 1989.

Habeck, M. *Storm of Steel. The Development of Armor Doctrine in Germany and the Soviet Union, 1919–1939.* Cornell University Press, 2003.

Le Donne, J. P. *The Grand Strategy of the Russian Empire, 1650–1831.* Oxford University Press, 2004.

Linn, B. *Guardians of Empire. The US Army in the Pacific, 1902–1940.* University of North Carolina Press, 1997.

Lupfer, T. T. *The Dynamics of Doctrine: The Changes in German Tactical Doctrine during the First World War.* Combat Studies Institute, US Army Command and General Staff College, 1981.

Luttwak, E. *The Grand Strategy of the Roman Empire.* Johns Hopkins University Press, 1979.

Mahan, A. T. *The Influence of Sea Power upon History, 1660–1789.* Pelican Publishing Company, 2003.

Malone, P. *The Skulking Way of War: Technology and Tactics Among the New England Indians.* Madison Books, 1993.

Mattern, S. *Rome and the Enemy: Imperial Strategy in the Principate.* University of California Press, 1998.

McElwee, W. *The Art of War: Waterloo to Mons.* Indiana University Press, 1974.

Miller, E. *War Plan Orange: The US Strategy to Defeat Japan, 1897–1945.* Naval Institute Press, 1991.

Mosier, J. *The Blitzkrieg Myth. How Hitler and the Allies Misread the Strategic Realities of World War II.* HarperCollins, 2003.

Muir, Rory. *Tactics and the Experience of Battle in the Age of Napoleon.* Yale University Press, 1998.

Murray, W., et al., eds. *The Making of Strategy: Rulers, States, and War.* Cambridge University Press, 1996.

Nafziger, G. *Imperial Bayonets.* Greenhill Books, 1996.

Nosworthy, B. *Anatomy of Victory: Battle Tactics 1689–1763.* Hippocrene Books, 1991.

Nosworthy, B. *With Musket, Cannon and Sword: Battle Tactics of Napoleon and His Enemies.* Sarpedon Publishers, 1996.

Paret, P., ed. *The Makers of Modern Strategy.* Princeton University Press, 1986.

Pearlman, M. *Warmaking and American Democracy: The Struggle Over Military Strategy, 1700 to the Present.* University Press of Kansas, 1999.

Posen, B. *The Sources of Military Doctrine: France, Britain and Germany between the World Wars.* Cornell University Press, 1984.

Ramsay, M. *Command or Cohesion: The Citizen Soldier and Minor Tactics in the British Army, 1870–1918.* Praeger Publishers, 2002.

Rogers, Clifford. *War Cruel and Sharp.* Boydell and Brewer, 2002.

Rosen, S. *Winning the Next War: Innovation and the Modern Military.* Cornell University Press, 1991.

Ross, S. *From Flintlock to Rifle: Infantry Tactics, 1740–1866.* Frank Cass Publishers, 1995.

Ross, Steven T. *American War Plans, 1941–1945: The Test of Battle.* International Specialized Book Services, 1997.

Rothenberg, G. E. *The Art of Warfare in the Age of Napoleon.* Indiana University Press, 1978.

Smail. R. C. *Crusading Warfare, 1097–1193.* Cambridge University Press, 1959.

Starr, C. *The Influence of Sea Power on Ancient History.* Oxford University Press, 1989.

Stoler, Mark. *Allies and Adversaries: The Joint Chiefs of Staff, the Grand Alliance, and US Strategy in World War II.* University of North Carolina Press, 2000.

Summers, H. G. *On Strategy: A Critical Analysis of the Vietnam War.* Presidio Press, 1982.

Verbruggen, J. F. *The Art of Warfare in Western Europe during the Middle Ages.* Boydell and Brewer, 1997.

Wilt. A. *War from the Top: German and British Military Decision Making during World War II.* Indiana University Press, 1990.

Zuber, T. *Inventing the Schlieffen Plan: German War Planning, 1871–1914.* Oxford University Press, 2003.

Institutional Military History

Baer, G. W. *One Hundred Years of Sea Power: The US Navy 1890–1990*. Stanford University Press, 1996.

Bartusis, M. *The Late Byzantine Army*. University of Pennsylvania Press, 1992.

Baxter, D. C. *Servants of the Sword: French Intendants of the Army, 1630–1670*. University of Illinois Press, 1976.

Braim, P. *The Test of Battle: The American Expeditionary Forces in the Meuse-Argonne Campaign*. White Mane Publishing Company, 1998.

Brewer, J. *The Sinews of Power. War, Money and the English State, 1688–1783*. Harvard University Press, 1988.

Brown, H. *War, Revolution, and the Bureaucratic State: Politics and Army Administration in France, 1791–1799*. Oxford University Press, 1995.

Dictionary of Military Terms: A Guide to the Language of Warfare and Military Institutions. Comp. Trevor N. Dupuy et al. H. W. Wilson, 2003.

Doubler, M. *Closing with the Enemy: How the GIs Fought the War in Europe, 1944–1945*. University Press of Kansas, 1995.

Elting, J. *Swords Around a Throne: Napoleon's Grande Armée*. Da Capo Press, 1989.

Fahmy, Khalid. *All the Pasha's Men: Mehmed Ali, His Army, and the Making of Modern Egypt*. American University in Cairo Press, 1997.

Farwell, B. *The Armies of the Raj*. W. W. Norton & Company, 1989.

Friday, K. *Hired Swords: The Rise of Private Warrior Power in Early Japan*. Stanford University Press, 1994.

Friday, K. *Samurai, Warfare and the State in Early Medieval Japan*. Routledge, 2004.

Goldsworthy, A. K. *The Roman Army at War*. Oxford University Press, 1998.

Graff, D. and R. Higham, eds. *A Military History of China*. Westview Press, 2002.

Hart, Russell. *Clash of Arms: How the Allies Won in Normandy*. University of Oklahoma Press, 2001.

Hewitt, H. J. *The Organization of War under Edward III*. Manchester University Press, 1958.

Hollister, C. W. *Anglo-Saxon Military Institutions on the Eve of the Norman Conquest*. Oxford University Press, 1962.

Hollister, C. W. *The Military Organization of Norman England*. Oxford University Press, 1964.

Howard, M. *The Causes of War and Other Essays.* T. Smith, 1984.

Humphreys, L. *The Way of the Heavenly Sword: The Japanese Army in the 1920s.* Stanford University Press, 1995.

Kennedy, Hugh. *The Armies of the Caliphs: Military and Society in the Early Islamic State.* Routledge, 2001.

Kennett, L. *The French Armies in the Seven Years War: A Study in Military Organization and Administration.* Duke University Press, 1967.

Keppie, L. *The Making of the Roman Army.* University of Oklahoma Press, 1997.

Le Bohec, Y. *The Imperial Roman Army.* Routledge, 1994.

Lone, S. *Army, Empire and Politics in Meiji Japan: the Three Careers of General Katsura Taro.* Palgrave Macmillan, 2000.

Lynn, J. *Bayonets of the Republic.* Westview Press, 1996.

Lynn, J. *The Giant of the Grand Siècle: The French Army 1610–1715.* Cambridge University Press, 1997.

Macksey, K. *Why The Germans Lose at War: The Myth of German Military Superiority.* Stackpole Books, 1999.

McGeer, E. *Sowing the Dragon's Teeth: Byzantine Warfare in the Tenth Century.* Dumbarton Oaks, 1995.

Menning, Bruce. W. *Bayonets before bullets: the Imperial Russian Army, 1861–1914.* Indiana University Press, 1992.

Moreman, T. R. *The Army in India and the Development of Frontier Warfare, 1849–1947.* Palgrave Macmillan, 1998.

Morillo, Stephen. *Warfare under the Anglo-Norman Kings, 1066–1135.* Boydell and Brewer, 1994.

Palmer, M. *Command at Sea: Naval Command and Control since the Sixteenth Century.* Harvard University Press, 2005.

Paret, P. *Yorck and the Era of Prussian Reform.* Princeton University Press, 1966.

Parker, H. M. D. *The Roman Legions.* Fromm International, 1928.

Prestwich, M. *Armies and Warfare in the Middle Ages: The English Experience.* Yale University Press, 1996.

Prucha, F. P. *The Sword of the Republic: The United States Army of the Frontier, 1783–1846.* University of Nebraska Press, 1987.

Ralston, D. *Importing the European Army.* University of Chicago Press, 1990.

Rossino, A. *Hitler Strikes Poland. Blitzkrieg, Ideology, Atrocity.* University Press of Kansas, 2003.

Rothenberg, Gunther. *The Army of Francis Joseph.* Purdue University Press, 1976.

Seaton, A. and J. Seaton. *The Soviet Army. 1918 to the Present.* New American Library, 1986.

Speidel, M. P. *Riding for Caesar: The Roman Emperors' Horse Guards.* Harvard University Press, 1994.

Treadgold, W. *Byzantium and its Army, 284–1081.* Stanford University Press, 1995.

War and Society

Abels, R. *Lordship and Military Obligation in Anglo-Saxon England.* University of California Press, 1988.

Anderson, M. S. *War and Society in Europe of the Old Regime, 1618–1789.* McGill-Queen's University Press, 1998.

Ayalon, D. *Gunpowder and Firearms in the Mameluke Kingdom.* Frank Cass Publishers; 2nd edition, 1978.

Bachrach, B. *Early Carolingian Warfare: Prelude to Empire.* University of Pennsylvania Press, 2001.

Barker, T. *Army, Aristocracy, Monarchy: Essays on War, Society, and Government in Austria, 1618–1780.* East European Monographs, 1982.

Best, G. *War and Society in Revolutionary Europe.* Palgrave Macmillan, 1982.

Bond, B. *War and Society in Europe, 1870–1970.* McGill-Queen's University Press, 1986.

Buckley, Roger Norman. *The British Army in the West Indies: Society and the Military in the Revolutionary Age.* University Press of Florida, 1998.

Chaniotis, A. *War in the Hellenistic World: A Social and Cultural History.* Blackwell Publishing, 2005.

Contamine, P. *War in the Middle Ages.* Trans. M. Jones. Blackwell Publishers, 1984.

Cotterell, A. *Chariot: The Astounding Rise and Fall of the World's First War Machine.* Overlook Hardcover, 2005.

De Pauw, L. G. *Battle Cries and Lullabies: Women in War from Prehistory to the Present.* University of Oklahoma Press, 1998.

Engels, D. *Alexander the Great and the Logistics of the Macedonian Army.* University of California Press, 1978.

Farris, W. W. *Heavenly Warriors: The Evolution of Japan's Military, 500–1300.* Harvard University Press, 1992.

Ferguson, N. *The Pity of War: Explaining World War I.* Basic Books, 2000.

Fischer, David Hackett. *Washington's Crossing.* Oxford University Press, 2004.

Forrest, A. *Conscripts and Deserters: The Army and French Society During the Revolution and Empire.* Oxford University Press, 1989.

France, J. *Western Warfare in the Age of the Crusades, 1000–1300.* Cornell University Press, 1999.

Haldon, J. *Warfare, State, and Society in the Byzantine World, 565–1204.* Routledge, 1999.

Hale, J. R. *War and Society in Renaissance Europe.* McGill-Queen's University Press, 1985.

Halsall, Guy. *Warfare and Society in the Barbarian West, 450–900.* Routledge, 2004.

Hanson, V. D. *The Western Way of War: Infantry Battle in Classical Greece.* University of California Press, 1989.

Hanson, V. D. *Carnage and Culture: Landmark Battles in the Rise of Western Power.* Anchor, 2002.

Hassig, R. *War and Society in Ancient Mesoamerica.* University of Oklahoma Press, 1992.

Howard, M. *War in European History.* Oxford University Press; new edn., 2001.

Goldsworthy, A. and I. Haynes. *Roman Army as a Community: Including Papers of a Conference Held at Birkbeck College, University of London, on 11–12 January 1997.* Journal of Roman Archaeology, 1999.

Lynn, J. ed. *Feeding Mars: Logistics in Western Warfare from the Middle Ages to the Present.* Westview Press, 1994.

Marwick, A. J. *War and Social Change in the Twentieth Century: A Comparative Study of Britain, France, Germany, Russia, and the United States.* Macmillan, 1974.

McNeill, W. *The Pursuit of Power.* University of Chicago Press, 1982.

McPherson, J. *Battle Cry of Freedom: The Civil War Era.* Oxford University Press, 1988.

McPherson, J. *What They Fought For, 1861–1865.* Anchor, 1995.

Neimeyer, Charles. *America Goes to War: A Social History of the Continental Army.* New York University Press, 1996.

Pennington, R. *Wings, Women, and War: Soviet Airwomen in World War II Combat.* University Press of Kansas, 2001.

Reynolds, S. *Fiefs and Vassals: The Medieval Evidence Reinterpreted.* Oxford University Press, 1996.

Rich, J. and G. Shipley, *War and Society in the Greek World.* Routledge, 1993.

Rich, J. and G. Shipley, *War and Society in the Roman World.* Routledge, 1993.

Rosen, S. *Societies and Military Power: India and its Armies.* Cornell University Press, 1996.

Smith, H. L. *War and Social Change: British Society in the Second World War.* Manchester University Press, 1986.

Speidel, M. P. *Ancient Germanic Warriors: Warrior Styles from Trajan's Column to Icelandic Sagas.* Routledge, 2004.

Strickland, Matthew. *War and Chivalry: The Conduct and Perception of War in England and Normandy, 1066–1217.* Cambridge University Press, 1996.

Tallett, F. *War and Society in Early Modern Europe, 1495–1715.* Routledge, 1992.

Van Creveld, M. *Supplying War: Logistics from Wallenstein to Patton.* Cambridge University Press, 1979.

Van Wees, H. *Greek Warfare. Myths and Realities.* Duckworth, 2004.

Wawro, G., *War and Society in Europe, 1792–1914.* Routledge, 2001.

Wells, D. and S. Wilson. *Russo-Japanese War in Cultural Perspective, 1904–05.* Palgrave Macmillan, 1999.

Whittow, M. *The Making of Orthodox Byzantium, 600–1025.* University of California Press, 1996.

RMAs, Technology and Military Transformation

Ayton, A. and J. L. Price. *The Medieval Military Revolution.* Barnes and Noble, 1996.

Barnett, Roger W. *Asymmetrical Warfare: Today's Challenge to US Military Power.* Potomac Books, 2000.

Barnett, Thomas P. M. *The Pentagon's New Map.* Putnam, 2004.

Black, J. *A Military Revolution? Military Change and European Society 1550–1800.* Palgrave Macmillan, 1991.

Black, J. *European Warfare 1660–1815.* Routledge, 1994.

Black, J. *War and the World, 1450–2000.* Yale University Press, 1998.

Brodie, B. *From Crossbow to H-bomb.* Indiana University Press, 1973.

Cipolla, C. *Guns, Sails, and Empires: Technological Innovation and the Early Phases of European Expansion, 1400–1700.* Sunflower University Press, 1965.

Cook, W. *The Hundred Years War for Morocco: Gunpowder and the Military Revolution in the Early Modern Muslim World.* Westview Press, 1994.

Drews, R. *Early Riders: The Beginnings of Mounted Warfare in Asia and Europe.* Routledge, 2004.

Drews, R. *The End of the Bronze Age: Changes in Warfare and the Catastrophe of ca. 1200 BC.* Princeton University Press, 1993.

Duffy, M. *The Military Revolution and the State, 1500–1800.* Humanities Press, 1980.

Eltis, D, *The Military Revolution in Sixteenth-Century Europe.* I. B. Tauris & Co Ltd, 1995.

Ferrill, A. *The Origins of War from the Stone Age to Alexander the Great.* Westview Press, 1985.

Glete, J. *War and the State in Early Modern Europe: Spain, the Dutch Republic and Sweden as Fiscal-military States, 1500–1660.* Routledge, 2001.

Gongoria, T. and H. von Rieckhoff. *Toward a Revolution in Military Affairs: Defense and Security at the Dawn of the Twenty-First Century.* Greenwood Press, 2000.

Guilmartin, J. *Gunpowder and Galleys: Changing Technology and Mediterranean Warfare at Sea in the Sixteenth Century.* Naval Institute Press, 1974.

Holm, J. *Women in the Military: An Unfinished Revolution.* Presidio Press, 1992.

Koburger, Jr., C. W. *Sea Power in the Twenty-First Century: Projecting a Naval Revolution.* Praeger Publishers, 1997.

Matthews, R. and J. Treddenick. *Managing the Revolution in Military Affairs.* Palgrave Macmillan, 2001.

Murray, W. and M. Knox, eds. *The Dynamics of Military Revolution, 1300–2050.* Cambridge University Press, 2001.

Murray, W. and A. Millett, eds. *Military Innovation in the Interwar Period.* Cambridge University Press, 1998

Parker, G. *The Military Revolution. Military Innovation and the Rise of the West 1500–1800.* Cambridge University Press, 1988, rev. 1996.

Perrin, N. *Giving Up the Gun: Japan's Reversion to the Sword, 1543–1879.* David R. Godine Publisher, 1995.

Rogers, C., ed. *The Military Revolution Debate.* Westview Press, 1996.

Schimmelpenninck van der Oye, D., et al., eds. *Reforming the Tsar's Army: Military Innovation in Imperial Russia from Peter the Great to the Revolution.* Cambridge University Press, 2004.

Van Creveld, M. *Technology and War.* Touchstone, 1989.

Wheeler, J. *The Making of a World Power: War and the Military Revolution in Seventeenth-Century England.* Sutton Publishing, 1999.

Other Perspectives and Disciplines

Archer, C. I., J. R. Ferris, et al., *World History of Warfare.* University of Nebraska Press, 2002.

Baynes, J. *Morale: A Study of Men and Courage.* Avery Publishing Group, 1967.

Black, J. *Rethinking Military History*. Routledge, 2004.

Blainey, G. *The Causes of War*. Free Press, 1988.

Bourke, J. *An Intimate History of Killing: Face-To-Face Killing in Twentieth-Century Warfare*. Basic Books, 1999.

Burke, P. *What is Cultural History?* Polity, 2004.

Cuneo, P. *Artful Armies, Beautiful Battles: Art and Warfare in Early Modern Europe*. Brill Academic Publishers, 2002.

Diamond, J. *Guns, Germs, and Steel: The Fates of Human Societies*. W. W. Norton & Company, 1997.

Dower, J. *War Without Mercy: Race and Power in the Pacific War*. Pantheon, 1986.

Ehrenreich, B. *Blood Rites: Origins and History of the Passions of War*. Owl Books, 1997.

Eisler, R. *The Chalice and the Blade*. Harper San Francisco, 1987.

Fenner, L. and M. de Young. *Women in Combat: Civic Duty or Military Liability?* Georgetown University Press, 2001.

Ferguson, B. and N. Whitehead, eds. *War in the Tribal Zone: Expanding States and Indigenous Warfare*. School of American Research Press, 1992.

Gilmore, A. *You Can't Fight Tanks with Bayonets: Psychological Warfare Against the Japanese Army in the Southwest Pacific*. University of Nebraska Press, 1998.

Grossman, D. *On Killing: The Psychological Cost of Learning to Kill in War and Society*. Back Bay Books, 1996.

Haas, J. *The Anthropology of War*. Cambridge University Press, 1990.

Keegan, J. *A History of Warfare*. Vintage, 1994.

Keeley, L. *War Before Civilization: The Myth of the Peaceful Savage*. Oxford University Press, 1996.

LeBlanc, S. and K. Register. *Constant Battles: The Myth of the Peaceful, Noble Savage*. St Martin's, 2003.

Lewis, M. E. *Sanctioned Violence in Early China*. State University of New York Press, 1990.

Lynn, J. *Battle: A History of Combat and Culture*. Perseus Books Group, 2003.

Mann, M. *The Sources of Social Power*. Cambridge University Press, 1986.

Marshall, S. L. A. *Men Against Fire*. University of Oklahoma Press, 1947.

Michno, G. F. *Lakota Noon: The Indian Narrative of Custer's Defeat*. Mountain Press, 1997.

Moran, Lord *The Anatomy of Courage*. Reprint edn., Avery, 1987.

Morillo, S., M. F. Pavkovic, and P. Lococo, *War in World History*.

Society, Technology and War from Ancient Times to the Present. McGraw-Hill, forthcoming.

Morrison, J. S., J. F. Coates, and N. B. Rankov. *The Athenian Trireme: The History and Reconstruction of an Ancient Greek Warship.* Cambridge University Press, 2000.

Munslow, A. *Deconstructing History.* Routledge, 1997.

Myerly, S. *British Military Spectacle from the Napoleonic Wars to the Crimea.* Harvard University Press, 1996.

O'Connell, R. *Of Arms and Men: A History of War, Weapons, and Aggression.* Oxford University Press, 1989.

O'Connell, R. *Ride of the Second Horseman. The Birth and Death of War.* Oxford University Press, 1995.

Paris, M. *Warrior Nation: Images of War in British Popular Culture, 1850–2000.* Reaktion Books Ltd, 2000.

Reyna, S. P. and R. E. Downs. eds. *Studying War: Anthropological Perspectives.* Gordon & Breach Science Publishing, 1994.

Scott, D. D., et al. *Archaeological Perspectives on the Battle of the Little Bighorn.* University of Oklahoma Press, 1989.

Scott, D. D., P. Willey, and M. A. Connor. *They Died with Custer. Soldiers' Bones from the Battle of the Little Bighorn.* University of Oklahoma Press, 1998.

Shay, Jonathan. *Achilles in Vietnam: Combat Trauma and the Undoing of Character.* Scribner, 1995.

Thomas, Emory. *Robert E. Lee: A Biography.* W. W. Norton, 1995.

Thordeman, B. and B. R. Price, *Armour from the Battle of Wisby.* Chivalry Bookshelf, 2001.

Tilly C. *Coercion, Capital, and European States, AD 990–1992.* Blackwell, 1990.

Index